THE
SAMKHYA PHILOSOPHY

CONTAINING

(1) SAMKHYA-PRAVACHANA SUTRAM, WITH THE VRITTI OF ANIRUDDHA, AND THE BHASYA OF VIJNANA BHIKSU AND EXTRACTS FROM THE VRITTI-SARA OF MAHADEVA VEDANTIN; (2) TATVA SAMASAY (3) SAMKHYA KARIKA; (4) PANCHASIKHA SUTRAM.

TRANSLATED BY

NANDALAL SINHA, M.A., B.L., P.C.S.

DEPUTY MAGISTRATE, DALTONGANJ.

KALPAZ

ISBN: 978-93-5128-870-1(PB)

First Published in 1915
Indian Reprint in 2017

Published by

Kalpaz Publications
C-30, Satyawati Nagar,
Delhi – 110052
E-mail: kalpaz@hotmail.com
Website: kalpazpublications.com
Ph.: +91-9212142040

Cataloging in Publication Data—DK
Courtesy: D.K. Agencies (P) Ltd. <docinfo@dkagencies.com>

Kapila, author.

The Samkhya philosophy : containing (1) Sâmkhya-pravachana sûtram, with the Vritti of Aniruddha, and the Bhâc ya of Vijnâna Bhikc u and extracts from the Vritti-sâra of Mahâdeva Vedantin (2) Tatva samâsa (3) Sâmkhya kârikâ (4) Panchaœikhâ sûtram / translated by Nandalal Sinha.

pages cm

English and Sanskrit.

Reprint. Originally published: Allahabad : Panini Office, 1915.

ISBN 9789351288701

1. Sankhya—Early works to 1800. I. Sinha, Nandalal, translator. II. Kapila. Sa˜n˜khyasu˜tra. III. Kapila. Sa˜n˜khyasu˜tra. English. IV. Title.

B133.K38S313 2017 DDC 181.41 23

THE SAMKHYA PHILOSOPHY

PREFACE.

The Contents of the Volume.

The present volume of the *Sacred Books of the Hindus* which bears the modest title of the *Sâṃkhya-Pravachana-Sûtram*, is, in reality, a collection of all the available original documents of the School of the Sâṃkhyas, with the single exception of the commentary composed by Vyâsa on the *Sâṃkhya-Pravachana-Yoga-Sûtram* of Patañjali. For it contains in its pages not only the *Sâṃkhya-Pravachana-Sûtram* of Kapila together with the *Vṛitti* of Aniruddha, the *Bhâṣya* of Vijñâna Bhikṣu, and extracts of the original portions from the *Vṛittisâra* of Vedântin Mahâdeva, but also the *Tattva-Samâsa* together with the commentary of Narendra, the *Sâṃkhya-Kârikâ* of Îśvarakṛiṣṇa with profuse annotations based on the *Bhâṣya* of Gauḍapâda and the *Tattva-Kaumudî* of Vâchaspati Miśra, and a few of the Aphorisms of Pañchaśikha with explanatory notes according to the *Yoga-Bhâṣya* which has quoted them. An attempt, moreover, has been made to make the volume useful in many other respects by the addition, for instance, of elaborate analytical tables of contents to the *Sâṃkhya-Pravachana-Sûtram* and the *Sâṃkhya-Kârikâ*, and of a number of important appendices.

In the preparation of this volume, I have derived very material help from the excellent editions of the *Vṛitti* of Aniruddha and the *Bhâṣya* of Vijñâna Bhikṣu on the *Sâṃkhya-Pravachana-Sûtram* by Dr. Richard Garbe, to whom my thanks are due. And, in general, I take this opportunity of acknowledging my indebtedness to all previous writers on the Sâṃkhya, living and dead, from whose writings I have obtained light and leading in many important matters connected with the subject.

An introduction only now remains to be written. It is proposed, however, to write a separate monogram on the Sâṃkhya Darśana, which would be historical, critical and comparative, in its scope and character. In this preface, therefore, only a very brief account is given of some of the cardinal doctrines of the Sâṃkhya School.

The Law of the Identity of Cause and Effect.

The first and foremost among these is the *Sat-Kârya-Siddhânta* or the Established Tenet of Existent Effect. It is the Law of the Identity of Cause and Effect: what is called the cause is the unmanifested state of what is called the effect, and what is called the effect is only the manifested state of what is called the cause; their substance is one and the same; differences of manifestation and non-manifestation give rise to the distinctions of Cause and Effect. The effect, therefore, is never non-existent; whether before its production, or whether after its destruction, it is always existent in the cause. For, nothing can come out of nothing, and nothing can altogether vanish out of existence.

Definition of Cause and Effect.

This doctrine would be better understood by a comparison with the contrary views held by other thinkers on the relation of cause and effect. But before we proceed to state these views, we should define the terms "cause" and "effect." One thing is said to be the cause of another thing, when the latter cannot be without the former. In its widest sense, the term, Cause, therefore, denotes an agent, an act, an instrument, a purpose, some material, time, and space. In fact, whatever makes the accomplishment of the effect possible, is one of its causes. And the immediate result of the operation of these causes, is their effect. Time and Space, however, are universal causes, inasmuch as they are presupposed in each and every act of causation. The remaining causes fall under the descriptions of "Material," "Efficient," "Formal," and "Final." The Sâṃkhyas further reduce them to two descriptions only, *viz.*, *Upâdâna*, *i.e.*, the material, which the Naiyâyikas call *Samavâyi* or Combinative or Constitutive, and *Nimitta*, *i. e.*, the efficient, formal, and final, which may be variously, though somewhat imperfectly, translated as the instrumental, efficient, occasional, or conditional, because it includes the instruments with which, the agent by which, the occasion on which, and the conditions under which, the act is performed. Obviously, there is a real distinction between the *Upâdâna* and the *Nimitta*: the *Upâdâna* enters into the constitution of the effect, and the power of taking the form of, in other words, the potentiality of being re-produced as, the effect, resides in it; while the *Nimitta*, by the exercise of an extraneous influence only, co-operates with the power inherent in the material, in its re-production in the form of the effect, and its causality ceases with such re-production. To take the case of a coin, for example: the material causality was in a lump of gold; it made possible the modification of the gold into the form of the coin, it will remain operative as long as the coin will last as a coin, and after its destruction, it will pass into the potential state again; but the operation of the *Nimittas* came to an end as soon as the coin was minted.

Aristotelian Division of Causes.

The Sâṃkhya Division.

Causes *Upâdâna* and *Nimitta* distinguished.

Similarly, the Sâṃkhyas distinguish the Effect under the twofold aspect of simple manifestation and of re-production. Thus, the coin is an instance of causation by re-production, while the production of cream from milk is an instance of causation by simple manifestation.

Theories of the Origin of the World.

Now, as to the origin of the world, there is a divergence of opinion among thinkers of different Schools: Some uphold the Theory of Creation, others maintain the Theory of Evolution. Among the Creationists are counted the Nâstikas or Nihilists, the Buddhists, and the Naiyâyikas; and among the Evolutionists, the Vedântins and the Sâṃkhyas. The Nâstikas hold that the world is non-existent, that is, unreal, and that it came out of what was not; the Buddhists hold that the world is existent, that is, real, and that it came out of what was not; the Naiyâyikas hold that the world is non-existent, that is, non-eternal, perishable, and that it came out of the existent, that is, what is eternal, imperishable; the Vedântins hold that the world is non-existent, that is, unreal, and that it came out of what was existent, that is, real, namely, *Brahman*; and the Sâṃkhyas hold that the world is existent, that is, real, and that it came out of what was existent, that is, real, namely, the *Pradhâna*. Thus, there are the *A-Sat-Kârya-Vâda* of the Nâstikas that a non-existent world has been produced from a non-existent cause, and of the Buddhists that an existent world has been produced from a non-existent cause, the *Abhâva-Utpatti-Vâda* of the Naiyâyikas that a non-eternal world has been produced from an eternal cause, the *Vivarta-Vâda* of the Vedântins that the world is a revolution, an illusory appearance, of the one eternal reality, *viz.*, *Brahman*, and the *Sat-Kârya-Vâda* of the Sâṃkhyas that an existent world has been produced from an existent cause.

Arguments which establish the Sâṃkhya Theory.

Against the theories of *A-Sat-Kârya*, *Abhâva-Utpatti*, and *Vivarta*, and in support of their theory of *Sat-Kârya*, the Sâṃkhyas advance the following arguments:

I. There can be no production of what is absolutely non-existent; *e.g.*, a man's horn.

II. There must be some determinate material cause for every product. Cream, for instance, can form on milk only, and never on water. Were it as absolutely non-existent in milk as it is in water, there would be no reason why it should form on milk, and not equally on water.

III. The relation of cause and effect is that of the producer and the produced, and the simplest conception of the cause as the producer is that it possesses the potentiality of becoming the effect, and this potentiality is nothing but the unrealised state of the effect.

IV. The effect is seen to possess the nature of the cause, *e.g.*, a coin still possesses the properties of the gold of which it is made.

V. Matter is indestructible; "destruction" means disappearance into the cause.

The World possesses phenomenal reality.

It follows, therefore, that cause and effect are neither absolutely dissimilar nor absolutely similar to each other. They possess *essential* similarities and *formal* dissimilarities. Such being the relation between cause and effect, the world cannot possibly have come out of something in which it had been absolutely non-existent, and which accordingly was, in relation to it, as good as non-existent. For the world is neither absolutely unreal nor absolutely real. The test of objective reality is its opposition to consciousness. It is distinguished as *Prâtibhâsika* or apparent, *Vyâvahârika* or practical or phenomenal, and *Pâramârthika* or transcendental. Of these, the world possesses phenomenal reality, and must, therefore, have a transcendental reality as its substratum. Thus is the Doctrine of *Sat-Kârya* established.

The Doctrine of Transformation.

A natural corollary from the above doctrine is the other doctrine of *Pariṇâma* or transformation. It is the doctrine that, as all effects are contained in their causes in an unmanifested form, the "production" of an effect is nothing but its manifestation, and that, as cause and effect are essentially identical, an effect is merely a transformation of the cause.

The Cause of the World, one or manifold?

Now, the question arises, whether the cause of the world be a single one, or whether it be manifold. Some think that, according to the Naiyâyikas, who declare the existence of *Parama-Aṇus* or the ordinary Atoms of Matter, the world has sprung from a plurality of causes. This is, however, to take a very superficial view of the Nyâya-Vaiśeṣika Darśana. The Naiyâyikas were certainly not timid explorers of metaphysical truths; there is absolutely no reason for supposing that they either would not or could not penetrate behind and beyond the ordinary Atoms of Matter. As I have elsewhere pointed out, it would be a mistake to treat the six Darśanas as each being a complete and self-contained system of thought; in respect of their scope and purpose, they bear no analogy to the philosophies of the West. They are singly neither universal nor final; but they mutually supplement one another. Their Risis address themselves to particular sets of people possessing different degrees of mental and spiritual advancement. They reveal

The Position of the Naiyâyikas explained.

and explain the truths embodied in the Vedas to them from their point of view and according to their competence, and thus help them in realising the truths for themselves and thereby in progressing towards Self-realisation. If the Naiyâyikas, therefore, do not carry their analysis of the world further than the ordinary Atoms of Matter, it must not be assumed that they teach a sort of atomic pluralism as the ultimate theory of the origin of the world, and are in this opposed to the authors of the other Śâstras which teach a different origin. The right explanation is that they make but a partial declaration of the Vedic truths and cut short the process of resolution at the ordinary Atoms of Matter, because they address themselves to a class of students who do not possess the mental capacity to grasp subtler truths.

Unity of the Cause of the World.

For the sense of unity which has found expression in the Law of Parsimony, points to a single original of the world or material manifestation, as revealed in the Vedas. And the Sâṃkhya makes its students acquainted with this. It is called the Root, and is described as the *Pradhâna,* that in which all things are contained, and as *Prakṛiti*, the mother of things.

The Scope of the Sâṃkhya.

It is a long way from the ordinary Atoms of Matter to the Pradhâna or Primordial Matter. The Sâṃkhya undertakes to declare and expound the successive transformations of the Pradhâna down to the Gross Matter, with the object of accomplishing the complete isolation of the Self from even the most shadowy conjunction with the Pradhâna.

Definition of Prakṛiti.

The definition of Prakṛiti is that it is the state of equilibrium of Sattva, Rajas, and Tamas, called the Guṇas. It is the genus of which the Guṇas are the species. Their state of equilibrium is their latent, potential, or inactive state, the state of not being developed into effects. The Guṇas are extremely fine substances, and are respectively the principles of illumination, evolution, and involution, and the causes of pleasure, pain, and dullness. For, Sattva is light and illuminating, Rajas is active and urgent, and Tamas is heavy and enveloping. They are in eternal and indissoluble conjunction with one another, and, by nature, mutually overpower, support, produce, and intimately mix with, one another.

The Doctrine of the Three Guṇas.

This doctrine of the Three Guṇas is the very foundation of the Sâṃkhya Tantra. It is explained in the following manner: (1) Everything in the world, external as well as internal, is in constant change; and there can be no change, whether it be movement in space, or whether it be movement in time, without rest. Side by side, therefore, with the principle of mutation, there must be a principle of conservation. And, as Berkeley tells us, existence is perception,--whatever is not manifested to Consciousness, individual or universal, does not exist. Another principle is, therefore, required which would make the manifestation of the other two principles and of their products, (as also of itself and of its own), to Consciousness possible. Thus, at the origin of the world, there must be a principle of conservation, a principle of mutation, and a principle of manifestation. (2) Similarly, an examination of the intra-organic energies would disclose the existence of three distinct principles behind them. These energies are the eleven Indriyas or Powers of Cognition and Action, and Prâṇa or Vital Force. Among them, the Powers of Cognition, *e.g.*, Seeing, Hearing, etc., cause manifestation of objects, the Powers of Action, *e.g.*, seizing by the hand, etc., produce change, and Prâṇa conserves and preserves life. (3) In the mind, again, modifications of three distinct characters take place; *viz.*, cognition, conation, and retention; and these could not be possible without there being a principle of manifestation, a principle of mutation, and a principle of conservation respectively. (4) Likewise, a psycho-æsthetic analysis of our worldly experience yields the result that everything in the universe possesses a threefold aspect, that is, it may manifest as agreeable, or as disagreeable, or as neutral, *i.e.*, neither agreeable nor disagreeable. It must then have derived these characteristics from its cause; for nothing can be in the effect which was not in the cause. The principles of manifestation, mutation, and conservation, therefore, which are operative in the change of the states of agreeable, disagreeable, and neutral, must also possess the nature of being pleasant (śânta), unpleasant (ghora), and dull (mûḍha).

It is these principles of manifestation, mutation, and conservation, possessing the nature of pleasure, pain, and dullness, that are respectively the Guṇas, Sattva, Rajas, and Tamas, of the Sâṃkhyas. They are the constitutive elements of Prakṛiti. They are Guṇas in their manifested forms; they are Prakṛiti in their unmanifested form.

The Transformations of Prakṛiti enumerated and distinguished.

The transformations of Prakṛiti are either *prakṛiti-vikṛiti*, original or evolvent as well as modification or evolute, or *vikṛiti*, modification or evolute merely. The former are themselves transformations of their antecedents, and, in their turn, give rise to subsequent transformations. They are Mahat, Ahaṃkâra, and the five Tan-mâtras. The latter are the eleven Indriyas and the five gross Elements. The transformation of Prakṛiti ceases with them. Of course, the gross Elements combine and evolve the material world ; but the world is not a different Tattva or principle from the Elements, because it does not develop a single attribute which is not already possessed by them. For the test of a Tattva or original or ultimate principle is that it possesses a characteristic property which is not possessed by any other Tattva.

The Objective World consists of Twenty-four Tattvas.

The objective world thus contains twenty-four Tattvas, namely, Prakṛiti, Mahat, Ahaṃ-kâra, Manas, the five Indriyas of Cognition, the five Indriyas of Action, the five Tan-mâtras, and the five gross Elements.

The Transformation of Prakṛiti is Mahat or Buddhi.

At the beginning of creation, there arises in Prakṛiti *Spandana* or cosmic vibration which disturbs its state of equilibrium, and releases the Guṇas from quiescence. Rajas at once acts upon Sattva and manifests it as Mahat. Mahat denotes Buddhi, the material counterpart and basis of what we term Understanding or Reason. Buddhi is called Mahat, great, because it is the principal among the Instruments of Cognition and Action. Mahat also means "light"; it is derived from the Vedic word *Mahas* or *Maghas*, meaning light. And Buddhi is called Mahat, because it is the initial transformation of Sattva which is the principle of manifestation. Or, Buddhi which is the first manifestation of the Guṇas and which is the material cause of the world, is called Mahat, in order to distinguish it from individual or finite Buddhis which are its parts. For "what is the Buddhi of the first-born golden-egged (Brahmâ), the same is the primary basis of all Buddhis; it is here called the 'great self.'"

Universal and Individual Buddhis distinguished.

Definition of Buddhi.

The function of Buddhi is *Adhyavasâya* or certainty leading to action. It manifests in eight forms; *viz.*, as virtue, knowledge, dispassion and power, while Sattva is predominant in it, and as vice, ignorance, passion, and weakness, while Tamas is predominant in it. And these, again, are modified into innumerable forms, which are classified as Error, Incapacity, Complacency, and Perfection. Such is Pratyaya-sarga or the creation of Buddhi or intellectual creation as contra-distinguished from elemental creation.

The Transformation of Buddhi is Ahaṃ-kâra.

From Buddhi springs Ahaṃ-kâra: from "*cogito*," I think, "*sum*," I am. Ahaṃ-kâra is literally the I-maker. It is the material counterpart and basis of what we term egoism, and causes modifications of Buddhi in the forms of "I am," "I do," etc., etc. It is the principle of personal identity and of individuation. Its function is *Abhimâna*, conceit, thinking with reference to itself, assumption of things to itself. But it is not a mere function; it is a substance in which reside *Vâsanâs* or the resultant tendencies of accumulated experience, and which is capable of modification into other and grosser forms.

Universal and Individual Aham-kâras distinguished.

This Aham-kâra, which is the first transformation of Buddhi, is the cosmic Aham-kâra, the Upâdhi or adjunct of the golden-egged Brahmâ, the Creator. It is the infinite source of the finite Aham-kâras of individual Jîvas.

The Transformations of Aham-kâra are: The Indriyas.

The modification of Aham-kâra is twofold, according as it is influenced by Sattva or by Tamas. The Sâttvic modifications are the eleven Indriyas, that is, the five Indriays of Cognition, *viz.*, the powers located in the Eye, Ear, Nose, Tongue, and Skin, the five Indriyas of Action, *viz.*, the powers located in the voice, hand, feet, and the organs of generation and of excretion, and Manas. Manas is both a power of cognition and a power of action. Assimilation and differentiation are its distinctive functions.

And the Tan-mâtras.

The Tâmasic modifications of Aham-kâra are the five Tan-mâtras, *viz.*, of Sound, Touch, Form, Flavour and Smell. They are pure, subtle or simple elements, the metaphysical parts of the ordinary Atoms of Matter. They are "fine substances," to quote from Vijñâna Bhikṣu, "the undifferentiated (a-viśeṣa) originals of the Gross Elements, which form the substratum of Sound, Touch, Form, Flavour and Smell, belonging to that class (that is, in that stage of their evolution) in which the distinctions of Śânta (pleasant), etc., do not exist." The process of their manifestation is as follows: The Tan-mâtra of Sound, possessing the attribute of Sound, is produced from Aham-kâra; then, from the Tan-mâtras of Sound, accompanied by Aham-kâra, is produced the Tan-mâtra of Touch, possessing the attributes of Sound and Touch. In a similar manner, the other Tan-mâtras are produced, in the order of their mention, by the addition of one more attribute at each successive step.

The Transformations of the Tan-mâtras are the Gross Elements.

The transformations of the Tan-mâtras are the Gross Elements of Ether, Air, Fire, Water, and Earth,—the ordinary Atoms of Matter, in which appear for the first time the distinctions of being pleasant, painful, and neutral. All Bodies, from that of Brahmâ down to a stock, are formed of them.

How the Existence of a Subjective Principle, Puruṣa, is explained.

Now, all this objective world is non-intelligent, because its material cause, Prakṛiti, is non-intelligent. It does not, therefore, exist or energise for its own sake. There must be some one else of a different nature, some intelligent being, for whose benefit, *i.e.*, experience and freedom, all this activity of Prakṛiti is. Thus do the Sâṃkhyas explain the existence of Puruṣa.

The Twentyfive Tattvas.

To classify the Tattvas logically, they may be exhibited thus :

- ***Jña.*** Knower, Intelligent, Subject : 25 Puruṣa.
- ***A-Jña.*** Non-knower, Non-intelligent, Object :
  - ***A-vyakta.*** Unmanifest : 24 Prakṛiti, the state of equilibrium of Sattva, Rajas and Tamas.
  - ***Vyakta.*** Manifest.
    - 23 Mahat.
      - 22 Aham-kâra.
        - × Sattva.
          - Indriyas of Cognition : Powers located in—
            - 20 The Eye.
            - 19 The Ear.
            - 18 The Nose.
            - 17 The Tongue.
            - 16 The Skin.
          - 21 Manas.
          - Indriyas of Action : Powers located in—
            - 15 Hands.
            - 14 Feet.
            - 13 Speech.
            - 12 Excretory Organ.
            - 11 Organ of generation.
        - × Tamas.
          - 10 Sound. — 9 Ether.
          - 8 Touch. — 7 Air.
          - 6 Form. — 5 Fire.
          - 4 Flavour. — 3 Water.
          - 2 Smell. — 1 Earth.

Of these, Puruṣa is the principle of Being, Prakṛiti is the principle of Becoming : Puruṣa eternally is, never becomes, while Prakṛiti is essentially Movement ; even during *Pralaya* or Cosmic Dissolution, its activity does not altogether cease ; it then undergoes homogeneous transformation : Sattva modifying as Sattva, Rajas modifying as Rajas, and Tamas modifying as Tamas. Puruṣa, on the other hand, is eternal consciousness undisturbed. Nothing can come into him, nothing can go out of him ; he is *Kûṭa-stha*, dwelling in the cave. And these two eternal co-ordinate principles are in eternal conjunction with each other. But conjunction as such does not set Prakṛiti in movement. Creation is caused by *Râga* or Passion. *Râga* is a change of state which spontaneously takes place in the Rajas of Buddhi, through the influence of Dharma and A-dharma. These are the natural consequences of the previous changes in the transformations of Prakṛiti,

Puruṣa and Prakṛiti contrasted.

The Spontaneity of Prakṛiti.

and they reside in Aham-kâra in the form of *Vâsanâ* or tendency, and render impure the Sattva of Buddhi. The activity of Prakṛiti, in the form of the disturbance of its Rajas element, is spontaneously evoked for the purpose of working out and exhausting the stored up Vâsanâ; its successive transformation is really a process of purification of the Sattva of Buddhi. This spontaneous tendency towards purification is due to the vicinity of Puruṣa.

The Nature of Puruṣa.

The Sâṃkhyas constantly hammer on the theme that no pain, no suffering, no bondage ever belongs to Puruṣa. Puruṣa is eternally free, never bound, never released. And because they thus thoroughly reveal the nature of Puruṣa, their doctrine is described as the Sâṃkhya, thorough-revealer.

The Meaning of the word, Sâṃkhya.

The "Bondage" of Puruṣa:

The "experience" of Puruṣa consists in his being the indifferent spectator of the changes that take place in Buddhi; his "bondage" is nothing but the reflection on him of the bondage, that is, the impurities, of Buddhi: his "release" is merely the removal of this reflection which, again, depends upon the recovery by Buddhi of its state of pristine purity, which means its dissolution into Prakṛiti. To say that the activity of Prakṛiti is for the benefit of Puruṣa is, therefore, a mere figure of speech. It is really for the purification of the Sattva of Buddhi.

Is due to A-vivaka.

To think, as people generally do. that pleasure and pain, release and bondage really belong to Puruṣa, is a mistake pure and simple. It is *A-vidyâ*. *A-viveka* is the cause of *A-vidyâ*. And *A-viveka*, non-discrimination, is the failure to discriminate Puruṣa from Prakṛiti and her products. Many are ignorant of the very existence of Puruṣa. Many are ignorant of his exact nature: some identify him with Prakṛiti, some with Mahat, some with Aham-kâra, and so on. Many, again, know the Tattvas in some form or other, but they know them not: knowledge, in the sense of mere information, they have, but no realisation, and it is realisation which matters. The Sâṃkhya, for this reason, enters into a detailed examination of the *Tattvas*, their number, nature, function, effect, inter-relation, resemblance, difference, etc., and insists on *Tattva-abhyâsa* or the habitual contemplation of the *Tattvas*, so that they may be *Sâkṣât-kṛita* or immediately known or realised. The way is also shown as to how, and the means, too, whereby, to discriminate, on the one hand, the gross Elements from the Tan-mâtras, the Tan-mâtras from the Indriyas, and both from Aham-kâra, Aham-kâra from Buddhi, and Buddhi

The Aim of the Sâṃkhya.

from Puruṣa, and, on the other hand, to discriminate Puruṣa from the gross and subtle Bodies and to prevent their further identification.

The Relation of the Yoga to the Sâṃkhya is that of Practice to Theory.

The Yoga which is the practice of the Sâṃkhya, which is the theory, takes up, and starts from, these central teachings of its predecessor, *viz.* (1) All activity—all change—is in and of Prakṛiti. (2) No activity—no change—is in Puruṣa. (3) The modifications of the mind are reflected in Puruṣa, and make him look like modified. (4) When the mind is calm and purified, Puruṣa shines as he really is. (5) Save and except these, reflection and its removal, bondage and release do not belong to Puruṣa. (6) Bondage and release are really of Prakṛiti, or, more strictly speaking, of the individualised form of its first transformation, *viz.*, Buddhi. From the point of view of the philosophy of the history of the Darśanas, these are the last words of the Sâṃkhya.

The Doctrine of the Subtle Body.

The Sâṃkhya also has brought the doctrine of Sûkṣma or Liṅga Śarîra, the Subtle Body, prominently to the fore. For, the purification of the Sattva of Buddhi may not be, and, as a general rule, is not, possible in one life, nor in one region of the Universe. But death seems to put an untimely end to the process of purification, by destroying the gross Body. How then can the process of purification be continued in other lives and in other regions? The Sâṃkhya replies that it can be and is so continued by means of the Subtile Body. It is composed of the seventeen *Tattvas,* beginning with Buddhi and ending with the Tan-mâtras. It is produced, at the beginning of Creation, one for each Puruṣa, and lasts till the time of Mahâ-Pralaya or the Great Dissolution. It is altogether unconfined, such that it may ascend to the sun dancing on its beams, and can penetrate through a mountain. And it transmigrates from one gross Body to another, from one region of the Universe to another, being perfumed with, and carrying the influence of, the *Bhâvas* or dispositions of Buddhi characterised as virtue, knowledge, dispassion, and power, and their opposites.

The Plurality of Puruṣas.

The Sâṃkhyas, again, teach a plurality of Puruṣas. This topic has been very fully discussed in the *Sâṃkhya-Pravachana-Sûtram*, I. 149-159, and the commentaries. Therein Vijñâna Bhikṣu has mercilessly criticised the doctrine of Non-duality maintained by some of the Vedântins, and has sought to establish the plurality of Puruṣas. And Garbe, in his characteristic style, contents himself with a flippant criticism of Vijñâna Bhikṣu's explanations. But Vijñâna Bhikṣu's criticisms are not aimed principally against the unity of Puruṣas, but at those interpretations of it, according to which the empirical Puruṣas, that is, mundane Puruṣas, the plurality of whom is established by irrefutable arguments, as in the Sâṃkhya Śâstra, are reduced to mere shadows without substance. He does not so much attack the unadulterated *A-Dvaita* of the Vedas and the Upaniṣats as its later developments. He was fully aware of the fact that none of the six Darśanas, for example, was, as we have hinted more than once, a complete system of philosophy in the Western sense, but merely a catechism explaining, and giving a reasoned account of, some of the truths revealed in the Vedas and Upaniṣats, to a particular class of students, confining the scope of its enquiry within the province of Creation, without attempting to solve to them the transcendental riddles of the Universe, which, in their particular stage of mental and spiritual development, it would have been impossible for them to grasp. Similarly, Garbe is wrong in thinking that Vijñâna Bhikṣu "explains away the doctrine of absolute monism." It is only a matter of interpretation and of stand-point; compare Râmânuja, Madhva, etc. For Vijñâna does not hesitate to do away even with the duality of Prakṛiti and Puruṣa when he observes that all the other *Tattvas* enter into absorption in Puruṣa and rest there in a subtle form, as does energy in that which possesses it. (*Vide* his Commentary on S-P-S., I. 61). For an explanation, therefore, of the apparent contradictions in the Darśanas, one must turn to the Vedas and Upaniṣats and writings of a similar scope and character. The Bhagavat-Gîtâ, for instance, declares :—

द्वाविमौ पुरुषौ लोके क्षरश्चाक्षर एव च ।
क्षरः सर्वाणि भूतानि कूटस्थोऽक्षर उच्यते ॥ १५ । १६ ॥
उत्तमः पुरुषस्त्वन्यः परमात्मेत्युदाहृतः ।
यो लोकत्रयमाविश्य बिभर्त्यव्यय ईश्वरः ॥ १५ । १७ ॥

In the world there are these two Puruṣas only, the mutable and the immutable. The mutable is all created things; the intelligent experiencer is said to be the immutable.—XV. 16.

While the highest Puruṣa is a different one, who (in the Upaniṣats) is called the Parama-Âtmâ, the Supreme Self, and who, presiding over the three worlds, preserves them, as the undecaying, omniscient, omnipotent Îśvara.—XV. 17.

Along such lines the so-called contradictions of the Darśanas find their reconciliation and true explanation in the higher teachings of the Upaniṣats.

The Sâṃkhya does not deny the Existence of God.

It will probably be contended that, in the case in question, such reconciliation is impossible in view of "one of the fundamental doctrines of the genuine Sâṃkhya, which is the denial of God" (Garbe). No graver blunder has ever been committed by any student of the Sâṃkhya! The genuine Sâṃkhya no more denies the existence of God than does Garbe's illustrious countryman, Emmanuel Kant, in his *Critique of Pure Reason.* To make this position clear, let us paraphrase the *Sâṃkhya-Pravachana-Sûtram* on the subject. Thus, Îśvara is not a subject of proof (I. 92). For, we must conceive Îśvara as being either *Mukta,* free, or *Baddha,* bound. He can be neither free nor bound; because, in the former case, being perfect, He would have nothing to fulfil by creation, and, in the latter case, He would not possess absolute power (I.93-94). No doubt, in the *Śrutis,* we find such declarations as "He is verily the all-knower, the creator of all," and the like; these, however, do not allude to an eternal, uncaused Îśvara (God), but are only eulogies of such Jîvas or Incarnate Selves as are going to be freed, or of the Yogins, human as well as super-human, who have attained perfection by the practice of Yoga (I. 95). Some say that attainment of the highest end results through absorption into the Cause (III. 54). But this is not so, because, as people rise up again after immersion into water, so do Puruṣas, merged into Prakṛiti at the time of *Pralaya,* appear, again, at the next Creation, as Îśvaras (III. 54-55). The Vedic declarations, *e. g.,* "He is verily the all-knower, the creator of all," refer to such Highest Selves (III. 56). Neither is the existence of God as the moral governor of the world, proved; for, if God Himself produce the consequences of acts, He would do so even without the aid of Karma; on the other hand, if His agency in this respect be subsidiary to that of Karma, then let Karma itself be the cause of its consequences; what is the use of a God? Moreover, it is impossible that God should be the dispenser of the consequences of acts. For, His motive will be either egoistic or altruistic. But it cannot be the latter, as it is simply inconceivable that one acting for the good of others, should create a world so full of pain. Nor can it be the former; because (1) in that case, He would possess unfulfilled desires, and, consequently, suffer pain and the like. Thus your worldly God would be no better than our Highest Selves. (2) Agency cannot be established in the absence of desire, for, behind every act, there lies an intense desire. And to attribute intense desire to God would be to take away from his eternal freedom. (3) Further, desire is a particular product of Prakṛiti. It cannot, therefore, naturally grow within the Self, whether it be God or the Jîva; it must come from the outside. Now, it cannot be said that desire, which is an evolute of Prakṛiti, directly has connection with the Self, as it would contradict hundreds of

Vedic declarations to the effect that the Self is *Asaṅga,* absolutely free from attachment or association. Neither can it be maintained that Prakṛiti establishes connection of desire with the Self by induction, as it were, through its mere proximity to it; as this would apply equally to all the Selves at the same time (V. 2-9). Furthermore, the above arguments might have lost their force or relevancy, were there positive proof of the existence of God; but there is no such proof. For, proof is of three kinds, *viz.*, Perception, Inference and Testimony. Now, God certainly is not an object of perception. Neither can He be known by Inference; because there is no general proposition (Vyâpti) whereby to infer the existence of God, inasmuch as, Prakṛiti alone being the cause of the world, the law of causation is of no avail here. And the testimony of the Veda speaks of Prakṛiti as being the origin of the world, and hence does not prove the existence of God (V. 10-12).

Thus the Sâṃkhyas maintain that it cannot be proved by evidence that an eternal, self-caused God exists: that the ordinary means of proof, Perception, Inference and Testimony, fail to reach Him; and that there is no other means of correct knowledge on our plane of the Universe. And when, therefore, Kapila thus declares that the various objective arguments for the establishment of theism, *viz.*, the ontological, the cosmological, the teleological, and the moral, cannot stand, and pronounces the verdict of 'non-proven' in regard to the existence of God, he takes up the right philosophical attitude, and there is absolutely no justification for branding his doctrine as atheistical merely on this score. "The notion that the existence of God is susceptible of dialectic demonstration has been surrendered, in later times," as Mr. Fitz-Edward Hall remarks, "by most Christian theologians of any credit: it now being, more ordinarily, maintained that our conviction of deity, on grounds apart from revelation, reposes solely on original consciousness, antecedent to all proof."

Thus the Sâṃkhya is *Nir-Îśvara*, but not *Nâstika.* It is not *Nâstika*, atheistical, because it does not deny the existence of God. It is *Nir-Îśvara, lit.* god-less, as it explains all and every fact of experience without reference to, and without invoking the intervention of a divine agency. Those who imagine that, in the Sâṃkhya, there is a denial of God, obviously fail to recognize the distinction between the two words, *Nâstika* and *Nir-Îśvara.* They, further, fail to bear in mind that the Sanskrit *Îśvara* and the English *God* are not synonymous terms. For, the opposite of *Nâstika* is *Âstika* (believer), one who believes in the existence of God, the authority of the

Nir-Îśvara and Nâstika are not convertible terms.

Veda, immortality, and so forth. Accordingly, the Hindu Darśanas have been classified as being either "*Âstika*" or "*Nâstika*," and the "*Nir-Îśvara*" Sâṃkhya has been always regarded as falling under the former category.

DALTONGANJ :

The 15th February, 1915. N. SINHA.

TABLE OF CONTENTS.

INTRODUCTORY.

BOOK IV : OF FABLES.

BOOK V: OF THE DEMOLITION OF COUNTER-THEORIES.

APPENDIX I.

INDEX OF APHORISMS.

APPENDIX II.

INDEX OF WORDS.

Word Index—Samkhya Pravachana Sutram.

य

Index of Words in Kapila Sutram (Tatva Samasa).

APPENDIX III.

INDEX OF AUTHORITIES QUOTED.

INDEX OF AUTHORITIES QUOTED.

***N.B.*—The numbers refer to the pages.**

APPENDIX IV.

A CATALOGUE OF SOME OF THE IMPORTANT WORKS ON THE SÂMKHYA.

A CATALOGUE OF SOME OF THE IMPORTANT WORKS ON THE SÂMKHYA.

A List of Recognised Text-Books of the Sâṃkhya School (Taken from Fitz-Edward Hall's Collection).

1. Sâṃkhya-Pravachana-Sûtram attributed to Ṛisi Kapila.
2. Sâṃkhya-Pravachana-Sûtra-Vṛitti by Aniruddha.
3. Sâṃkhya-Pravachana-Sûtra-Vṛitti-Sârah by Mahâdeva Sarasvati, more commonly known as Vedântin Mahâdeva.
4. Sâṃkhya-Pravachana-Bhâṣyam by Vijñâna Bhikṣu.
5. Lagbu-Sâṃkhya-Sûtra-Vṛitti by Nâgoji Bhatta or Nâgeśa Bhatta, surnamed as Upâdhyâya.
6. Tattva-Samâsaḥ, attributed to Ṛisi Kapila.
7. Sâṃkhya-Taraṅgaḥ, a Commentary on No. 1, by Viśveśvaradatta Miśra, ascetically called Deva Tîrtha.
8. Sarvopakâriṇî, a Commentary on No. 6. Author is not known.
9. Sâṃkhya-Sûtra-Vivaraṇam, ditto. ditto.
10. Sâṃkhya-Krama-Dîpikâ, also called Sâṃkhyalaṅkarah and Sâṃkhya-Sûtra-Prakṣepikâ, ditto. ditto.
11. Tattva-Yâthârthya-Dîpanam, ditto, by Bhâvâ Ganeśa Dîkṣita.
12. Tattva-Samâsa-Vyâkhyâ, by Kṣemânanda.
13. Sâṃkhya-Kârikâ, also called Saptatih, by Îśvara Kṛiṣṇa.
14. Sâṃkhya-Karikâ-Bhâṣyam, by Gauḍapâda.
15. Sâṃkhya-Tattva-Kaumudî, shortly called Tattva-Kaumudî, by Vâchaspati Miśra.
16. An exposition of No. 14, by Yati Bhâratî.
17. Tattvârnavaḥ, otherwise called Tattvâmṛita-Prakṣinî, a Commentary on No. 14, by Râghavânanda Sarasvatî.
18. Tattva-Chandraḥ, ditto, by Nârâyaṇa Tîrtha Yati.
19. Kaumudî-Prabhâ, ditto, by Svapneśvara.
20. Sâṃkhya-Tattva-Vilâsaḥ, also called Sâṃkhya-Vṛitti-Prakâśaḥ and Sâṃkhyârtha-Sâṃkhyâyikâ, by Raghunâtha Tarka Vâgîśa Bhaṭṭâchârya.
21. Sâṃkhya-Chandrikâ, a Commentary on No. 12, by Nârâyaṇa Tîrtha.
22. Sâṃkhya-Sâra-Vivekaḥ, by Vijñâna Bhikṣu.
23. Sâṃkhya-Tattva-Pradîpaḥ, by Kavirâja Yati or Kavirâja Bhikṣu.
24. Sâṃkhyârtha-Tattva-Pradîpikâ, by Bhatta Keśava.
25. Sâṃkhya-Tattva-Vibhâkaraḥ, perhaps by Vansîdhara.
26. Sâṃkhya-Kaumudî, by Râmkṛiṣṇa Bhaṭṭâchârya.
27. Râja-Vârtikam, attributed to Raṇaraṅga Malla, king of Dhârâ.

APPENDIX V.

TATTVA-SAMÂSA OR KÂPILA-SÛTRAM.

APPENDIX VI.

SÂMKHYA-KÂRIKÂ OF ISVARAKṚIṢṆA.

TABLE OF CONTENTS.

THE SÂMKHYA-KÂRIKÂ.

The Sâṃkhya is the only means of the Supreme Good.

दुःखत्रयाभिघातात् जिज्ञासा तदवघातके हेतौ ।
दृष्टे सापार्था चेन्नैकान्तात्यन्ततोऽभावात् ॥ १ ॥

दुःखत्रयाभिघातात् Duḥkha-traya-abhighâtât, from the disagreeable occurrence, affection or action (abhighâta) of the threefold pain or causes of suffering. जिज्ञासा Jijñâsâ, the desire to know, enquiry. तदवघातके Tat-avaghâtake, preventive or counter-active thereof, *i.e.*, of the threefold pain. हेतौ Hetau, into the means. दृष्टे Driṣṭe, there existing visible or ordinary means. सा Sâ, it, *i.e.*, the enquiry. अपार्थी Apa-arthâ, purpose-less, superfluous. चेत् Chet, if it is said. न Na, no. एकान्तात्यन्ततोऽभावात् Ekânta-atyanta-taḥ-abhâvât, because of the absence of certainty and permanency.

I. From the disagreeable occurrence of the threefold pain, (proceeds) the enquiry into the means which can prevent it; nor is the enquiry superfluous because ordinary (means) exist, for they fail to accomplish certain and permanent prevention of pain.

ANNOTATION.

1. Wise men want to demonstrate that which, by being known, would accomplish the Supreme Good. Knowledge about the subject matter of the proposed Śâstra is the means of accomplishing the Supreme Good. The present Kârikâ, therefore, introduces an enquiry into that subject.—Vâchaspati Miśra's *Tattva-Kaumudî*.

2. The subject-matter of the Sâṃkhya System comprises the well-known Twenty-five Tattvas or Principles, from the knowledge of which results the destruction of the three kinds of pain. Cf. Gauḍpâda's *Bhâṣyam*.

3. The Supreme Good is Mokṣa or Release which consists in the permanent impossibility of the incidence of pain in any form whatever, that is, in recovering that state of the pristine purity of the Self in which the occurrence of pain is impossible, in other words, in the realisation of the Self as Self pure and simple.

4. Pains, according to the place of their origin, are divided primarily into two classes: internal and external. Internal pains, again, are either bodily or mental. These are called Âdhyâtmika or intra-organic. External pains are either Âdhibhautika or caused by created beings, namely, man, beast, bird, reptile, and the immobile, or Âdhidaivika or caused by supernatural agencies, such as Yakṣa, Râkṣasa, Vinâyaka, etc. Now, pain, such as it is, cannot be ignored, because it is experienced by every individual being.

5. Pain is not a condition of the pure Self. It resides in the Internal Instrument of Action and Cognition, that is, the inner sense, or Buddhi, and is a particular modification of that component element of it which is called Rajas. "Abhighâta" is the contact of the power of Sentiency with pain as an object of disagreeable sensation.

6. It may be objected that when such obvious remedies as medicines, desirable objects, skill in political arts and sciences, employment of gems and charms, etc., for the alleviation and removal of pain, do exist, whilst the knowledge of the Tattvas is difficult of attainment and to be acquired only by long study and traditional tuition through many generations, the investigation proposed is needless. To this, the answer is that the obvious means are neither Ekânta or absolute, nor Atyanta or final; that is, there is in them no certainty of the cessation of pain nor of the non-recurrence of pain that has ceased. Therefore, the good accomplished by them is not the Supreme Good. The means of accomplishing the Supreme Good must possess these two properties. Such a means is the knowledge of the Tattvas. The enquiry, therefore, is certainly not needless.

7. But our opponent may contend that, though the obvious means may fail, still there are means declared in the Vedas, which bring about absolute and final cessation of pain, and that, consequently, the proposed enquiry is quite superfluous. Accordingly, the next Kârikâ declares:

Scriptural, like ordinary, means are defective.

दृष्टवदानुश्रविकः सह्यविशुद्धिक्षयातिशययुक्तः ।
तद्विपरीतः श्रेयान् व्यक्ताव्यक्तज्ञविज्ञानात् ॥ २ ॥

दृष्टवत् Driṣṭa-vat, like the ordinary (means). आनुश्रविकः Ânuśravikaḥ, the revealed, Vedic, scriptural. सः Saḥ, it, *i.e.*, the Vedic means. हि Hi, for. अविशुद्धिक्षयातिशययुक्तः A-viśuddhi-kṣaya-atiśaya-yuktaḥ, attended with impurity, waste, and excess. तद्विपरीतः Tat-viparîtaḥ, the opposite thereof, *i.e.*, of ordinary and scriptural means. श्रेयान् Śreyân, preferable. व्यक्ताव्यक्तज्ञविज्ञानात् Vyakta-a-vyakta-jña-vijñânât, as it consists in discriminative knowledge of the Manifest, the Unmanifest, and the Knower.

II. Like the ordinary, is the scriptural (means ineffectual), for it is attended with impurity, waste, and excess. (The means which is) the opposite of both is preferable, as it consists in a discriminative knowledge of the Manifest, the Unmanifest, and the Knower.

ANNOTATION.

8. "Scriptural" here refers to the rituals laid down in the Vedas, and not to their Jñâna-Kâṇḍa portion, for Discriminative Knowledge also is enjoined in them.

The scriptural means are, *e.g.*, the drinking of the Soma juice, performance of sacrifices such as the Jyotiṣṭoma, the Aśvamedha, etc. They are "impure" from sacrifice of animals, etc. The result produced by them is liable to "waste," for even heaven and the gods pass away in course of time. They are also inequal in the distribution of their rewards.

9. The "opposite of both" that is, that which is absolute and final in its result, and is free from impurity, deficiency, and inequality. Such a means is the discriminative knowledge of Prakṛiti and Puruṣa.

10. "Vijñâna" means knowledge of discrimination. Knowledge of the Manifest leads to the knowledge of its cause, the Unmanifest. And knowledge of both as existing for the sake of another, leads to the knowledge of the Self. The Manifest begins with Mahat and includes Ahaṃkâra, the five Tan-mâtras, the eleven Indriyas, and the five Great Elements. The Unmanifest is the Pradhâna, *i.e.*, Prakṛiti. The Knower is Puruṣa. These are the Twenty-five Tattvas.

11. The mutual differences of the Manifest, the Unmanifest, and the Knower are declared in the next Kârikâ.

The Manifest, the Unmanifest, and the Knower distinguished.

मूलप्रकृतिरविकृतिर्महदाद्याः प्रकृतिविकृतयः सप्त ।
षोड़शकस्तु विकारः न प्रकृतिर्न विकृतिः पुरुषः ॥ ३ ॥

मूलप्रकृतिः Mûla-prakṛitiḥ the root-evolvent. अविकृतिः A-vikṛitiḥ, non-evolute. महदाद्याः Mahat-âdyâḥ, Mahat, etc. प्रकृतिविकृतयः Prakṛiti-vikṛitayaḥ, evolvent-evolutes. सप्त Sapta, seven. षोडशकः Ṣodaśakaḥ, sixteen. तु Tu, merely. विकारः Vikâraḥ, evolute. न Na, not. प्रकृतिः Prakṛitiḥ, evolvent. न Na, not. विकृति : Vikṛitiḥ, evolute. पुरुषः Puruṣaḥ, Puruṣa.

III. The Root Evolvent is no evolute ; Mahat, etc., are the seven evolvent-evolutes ; the sixteen are mere evolutes ; (that which is) neither evolvent nor evolute, is Puruṣa.

12. By "Prakṛiti" is meant that which procreates or evolves—the Pradhâna, that is, that in which all things are contained, and in its general significance, it denotes that which becomes the material cause of another Tattva.

13. The Root Evolvent is the state of equipoise of Sattva, Rajas, and Tamas. It has no root of its own and is the root of all things. Hence it is not a product. To imagine a root for the Root Evolvent would entail infinite regression.

14. Evolvent-Evolutes : Mahat springs from the Pradhâna and, in its turn, gives rise to Ahaṃkâra ; Ahaṃkâra, in its turn, to the Tan-mâtras of Sound, Touch, Smell, Form, and Taste ; and these, in their turn, respectively to the gross elements of Ether, Air, Earth, Fire, and Water.

15. It is next to be considered how the existence of the Tattvas described above can be rationally established. The causes of cognition and non-cognition are, therefore, expounded in the following four Kârikâs.

Sources of knowledge enumerated.

दृष्टमनुमानमाप्तवचनं च सर्वप्रमाणसिद्धत्वात् ।
त्रिविधं प्रमाणमिष्टं प्रमेयसिद्धिः प्रमाणाद्धि ॥ ४ ॥

दृष्टम् Dristam, the seen, sensuous, perception. अनुमानम् Anumânam, inference. आप्तवचनं Âpta-vachanam, statement of trustworthy persons. च Cha, and. सर्वप्रमाणसिद्धत्वात् Sarva-pramâna-siddha-tvât, because all proofs are established. त्रिविधं Tri-vidham, threefold. प्रमाणम् Pramâṇam, proof. इष्टं Iṣtam, desired. प्रमेयसिद्धिः Prameya-siddhiḥ, establishment of the existence of the things to be proven, *viz.*, the Twenty-five Tattvas. प्रमाणात् Pramâṇât, from proof. हि Hi, verily.

IV. Perception, Inference, and Testimony (are the Proofs ; by these) all proofs being established, Proof is intended to be threefold. From Proof verily is the establishment of the Provables.

Perception, Inference, and Testimony defined.

प्रतिविषयाध्यवसायो दृष्टं त्रिविधमनुमानमाख्यातम् ।
तल्लिङ्गलिङ्गिपूर्वकमाप्तश्रुतिराप्तवचनन्तु ॥ ५ ॥

प्रतिविषयाध्यवसाय: Prati-viṣaya-adhyavaṣâyaḥ, ascertainment of each respective object by the senses. दृष्टं Dristam, perception. त्रिविधम् Trividham, threefold. अनुमानम्-

Anumânam, inference. आख्यातम् Âkhyâtam, declared. तत् Tat, it. लिङ्गलिङ्गिपूर्वकम् Linga lingi-pûrvakaṃ, preceded by the mark and by that of which it is the mark. आप्तश्रुतिः Âpta-śrutiḥ, trustworthy person and the Veda. आप्तवचनं Âpta-vachanam, trustworthy statement, testimony. तु Tu, while.

V. Perception is the ascertainment of each respective object (by the Senses). Inference has been declared to be threefold. It is preceded by the mark and it is preceded by the thing of which it is the mark. While Testimony is the statement of trustworthy persons and the Veda.

ANNOTATION.

16. Vâchaspati Miśra interprets "Prati-viṣaya-adhyavaṣâyaḥ" as follows: Adhyavaṣâya, that is, the operation of Buddhi, in other words, cognition, based on or depending upon Prati-viṣaya, that is, that which functions in regard to, that is, comes into contact with, the several objects, in other words, the Senses.

17. The same authority describes the process of perceptual cognition thus: On the modification of the Senses apprehending objects, when there takes place the subdual of the Tamas of Buddhi, there is predominance of the Sattva, which is variously called Adhyavaṣâya, Vṛitti, and Jñâna. And the favour that is hereby done to the power of intelligence, that is the fruit; it is the consciousness of Pramâ or Right Cognition. For the Buddhi Tattva, being derived from Prakṛiti, is unintelligent; hence its Adhyavaṣâya also is unintelligent, like a jar, etc. Similarly, the other modifications of the Buddhi Tattva, such as pleasure, etc., also are unintelligent. While Puruṣa, unassociated with pleasure, etc., is intelligent. Yet he, by the falling of the shadow of cognition, pleasure, etc., reflected by those residing in the Buddhi Tattva, becomes, as though possessed of cognition, pleasure, etc. This is how the intelligent one is favoured. And by the falling of the shadow of intelligence, Buddhi and also its Adhyavaṣâya, though unintelligent, appear, as though intelligent.

18. Anumâna is inference, by means of the mark, of the thing of which it is the mark, and *vice versâ*. The Methods of Inference are either of Agreement, called Vîta, or of Difference, called A-Vîta. A-Vîta inference is called Śeṣa-vat, because it has the Śeṣa or the remainder or the residue as its subject matter. *E.g.*, Earth is not not-Earth, because it possesses smell. Gauḍapâda explains Śeṣa-vat to be inference in respect of the Śeṣa or remainder of the class; *e.g.*, having found a drop of water taken from the sea to be salt, the saltness of the rest also is inferred.

Vîta inference is two-fold: Pûrva-vat and Sâmânyato Drișța. Pûrva-vat is the inference of an individual of a genus particular instances of which have previously been seen; *e.g.*, the inference of fire from smoke, in a mountain, fire having previously been seen in the kitchen. Sâmânyato Drișța is inference of a thing particular instances of which same kind have not previously been seen, but particular instances of a kind similar to which have previously been seen in analogous cases; that is, in this case, the particular is not seen but the genus is seen. *E.g.*, Karaṇa-tva or instrumentality, that is, the capability of effecting an act is, as a genus, a known thing, because it has been seen in the axe which is an instrument of cutting. But an Indriya or Power of Cognition and Action (commonly rendered as Sense Organ) does not belong to the same class as the axe, and is also not an object of perception. Now, cognition and action are acts, and as the act of cutting cannot be effected without an instrument, so the acts of cognition and action cannot be effected without some instrument. Thus is inferred the existence of the Indriyas as the Instruments of Cognition and Action.

Âpta means Âchâryas, such as Brahmâ and the rest.

Super-Sensible objects how proved.

सामान्यतस्तु दृष्टादतीन्द्रियाणां प्रतीतिरनुमानात् ।
तस्मादपि चासिद्धं परोक्षमाप्तागमात् सिद्धम् ॥ ६ ॥

सामान्यत: Sâmânyataḥ, of the generic. तु Tu, but. दृष्टात् Drișțât, from the seeing. अतीन्द्रियाणां Ati-indriyâṇâm, of things transcending the senses. प्रतीति: Pratîtiḥ, approach, intuition, cognition. अनुमानात् Anumânât, from inference. तस्मात् Tasmât, from that. अपि Api, even. च Cha, and also, from Śeșa-vat inference (Vâchaspati). असिद्धं A-siddham, not-established. परोक्षम् Parokșam, super-sensuous. आप्तागमात् Âpta-âgamât, from Testimony and Revelation. सिद्धम् Siddham, proved.

VI. (Intuition of sensible things is from perception). But the intuition of super-sensible things is from Sâmânyato Drișța and Seșa-vat Inference. And super-sensible things not established from that even, are established from Testimony and Revelation.

19. Prakriti and Puruṣa are not objects of perception and therefore they are unreal, argue our opponents; for a hare's horn or a castle in the air is not perceived, because it is unreal. It is, accordingly, next pointed out that perception cannot be the sole test of reality, because there are well-known causes from which even admittedly existent things are not perceived. These causes are declared in the next Kârikâ.

Causes of failure of external perception enumerated.

अतिदूरात् सामीप्यादिन्द्रियघातान्मनोऽनवस्थानात् ।
सौक्ष्म्याद्व्यवधानादभिभवात् समानाभिहाराच्च ॥ ७ ॥

अतिदूरात् Ati-dûrât, from extreme distance. *N.B.*—The word Ati qualifies distance as well as all the rest. सामीप्यात् Sâmîpyât, from nearness. इन्द्रियघातात् Indriya-ghâtât, from impairment of the senses. मनोऽनवस्थानात् Manaḥ-anavasthânât, from non-presence of mind. सौक्ष्म्यात् Saukṣmyât, from fineness. व्यवधानात् Vyavadhânât, from intervention. अभिभवात् Abhibhavât, from suppression by others. समानाभिहारात् Samâna-abhihârât, from intermixture with likes. च Cha, and others.

VII. (Apprehension of even existing things may not take place) through extreme remoteness, nearness, impairment of the senses, non-presence of the mind, extreme fineness, intervention, suppression by other matters, intermixture with likes, and other causes.

Why Prakṛiti is not an object of perception.

सौक्ष्म्यात्तदनुपलब्धिर्नाभावात् कार्यतस्तदुपलब्धेः ।
महदादि तच्च कार्यं प्रकृतिसरूपं विरूपं च ॥ ८ ॥

सौक्ष्म्यात् Saukṣmyât, from extreme fineness. तदनुपलब्धिः Tat-anupalabdhiḥ, non-apprehension thereof, *i.e.*, of Prakṛiti. न Na, not. अभावात् Abhâvât, from non-existence. कार्यतः Kârya-taḥ, from effects. तदुपलब्धेः Tat-upalabdheḥ, because of the apprehension thereof. महदादि Mahat-âdi, Mahat and the rest. तत् Tat, that. च Cha, and. कार्यं Kâryaṃ, effect. प्रकृतिसरूपं Prakṛiti-sarûpaṃ, similar to Prakṛiti. विरूपं Virûpaṃ, dissimilar. च Cha, and.

VIII. From extreme fineness is the non-apprehension of Prakṛiti, and not from her non-existence, because there is apprehension of her from the effect. And that effect is Mahat, etc., similar and dissimilar to Prakṛiti.

20. "Similar and dissimilar to Prakṛiti": for these resemblances and differences, see Kârikâs X and XI.

21. But from the effects, a mere cause or cause in the abstract is deduced, and not its nature, and, on this point, different conclusions have been arrived at by different thinkers. Thus, some Buddhists, say that the existent is produced from the non-existent; *e.g.*, from the non-existence, by destruction, of the seed is produced the sprout. 2. Some, the Vedântins, say that the effects are the Vivarta or revolution of one

single existent thing, and are not themselves ultimately real. 3. Some, the Vaiśeṣikas, Naiyâyikas, etc., say that from the existent, *i.e.*, the Ultimate Atoms, is produced the non-existent. 4. The elders, the Sâṃkhyas, say that from the existent is produced the existent. Of these, on the first three alternatives, the Pradhâna is not established. For the characteristic of being the Pradhâna, *i.e.*, that in which all things are contained, and of being of the nature of Sattva, Rajas and Tamas, belonging to the Cause of the World, consists in being of the nature of Sound and all other Pariṇâma or transformations, the essences of which possess the distinctions of pleasure, pain, and bewilderment. Now, if the existent is to be produced from the non-existent, how can a non-existent, nameless, form-less cause possess the nature of Sound, etc., in the form of pleasure, etc.? for there is no proof of the identity of nature between the existent and the non-existent. If, again, the diversity of Sound, etc., is the Vivarta of a single existent thing, still it would not follow that the existent is produced from the existent. For a one without a second cannot have identity of nature with the diversity; on the contrary, the apprehension of the non-diversity under the characteristic of the diversity is an error pure and simple. With those also, again, namely Kaṇâda, Gotama, and others, who say that it is from the existent that the non-existent is produced, the cause cannot be of the nature of the effect, because there is no proof of the unity of the existent and the non-existent. Hence there can be no proof of the Pradhâna on these theories. In order, therefore, to establish the existence of the Pradhâna, the next Kârikâ determines that the effect must be existent from before its "productfon."

Effects pre-exist in their causes.

असदकरणादुपादानग्रहणात् सर्वसम्भवाभावात् ।
शक्तस्य शक्यकरणात् कारणभावाच्च सत् कार्यम् ॥ ९ ॥

असदकरणात् A-sat-a-karaṇât, from the non-effectuation of the non-existent. उपादानग्रहणात् Upâdâna-grahaṇât, from the selection of material for the effect. सर्वसम्भवाभावात् Sarva-sambhava-abhâvât, from the absence of the production of every thing by every means. शक्तस्य Śaktasya, of the competent. शक्यकरणात् Śakya-karaṇât, from the effectuation of the producible. कारणभावात् Kâraṇa-bhâvât, from the nature of the cause. सत् Sat, existent. कार्यम् Kâryam, effect.

IX. The effect is ever existent, because that which is non-existent, can by no means be brought into existence; because effects take adequate material causes; because all things are not produced from all causes ; because a competent cause can effect that only for which it is competent; and also because the effect possesses the nature of the cause.

ANNOTATION.

22. That which is non-existent, etc. : *e.g.* a hare's horn.

Effects take, etc. : Oil, for instance, can be produced from mustard seeds, but not a piece of cloth.

All things are not produced, etc. : Did effects not pre-exist in their causes, then, in mustard seeds, for example, there would be non-existence of a piece of cloth, a jar, in fact, of every other thing as well as of oil, and it would be quite as easy to produce a piece of cloth, a jar, and all the rest from them as it is to produce oil. But such is not the case.

A competent cause can effect, etc. : Competency means potentiality, the unmanifested state of the effect. A lump of clay, for instance, is potentially a jar ; in it the jar lies hidden, unmanifested ; it is manifested in the form of the jar by the operation of the potter.

The effect possesses the nature, etc. : The colour, weight, touch, etc. of a piece of cloth for instance, are the colour, weight, touch, etc., of the threads from which it is made. This could not have been so, were not cause and effect identical in essence.

The Manifest and the Unmanifest contrasted.

हेतुमदनित्यमव्यापि सक्रियमनेकमाश्रितं लिङ्गम् ।
सावयवं परतन्त्रं व्यक्तं विपरीतमव्यक्तम् ॥ १० ॥

हेतुमत् Hetu-mat, possessing or depending on a cause. अनित्यम् A-nityam, non-eternal, perishable. अव्यापि A-vyâpi, unpervading, finite. सक्रियम् Sakriyam, mobile, mutable. अनेकम् Anekam, multitudinous, manifold. आश्रितं Âśritam, supported, dependent. लिङ्गम् Lingam, mergent, mark. सावयवं Sâvayavam, made up of parts. परतन्त्रं Para-tantram, subordinate. व्यक्तं Vyaktam, the manifested. विपरीतम् Viparîtam, the reverse. अव्यक्तम् A-Vyaktam, the unmanifested.

X. The Manifest is producible, non-enternal, non-pervading, mobile, multiform, dependent, (serving as) the mark (of inference), a combination of parts, subordinate. The Unmanifest is the reverse (of this).

ANNOTATION.

23. *Sakriya*, migratory : Buddhi and the rest leave, one after another, bodies which they had taken up and enter into other bodies : this is their movement. The movement of the Body, Earth, etc., is indeed well-known.

Aneka, multitudinous : There are as many of them as there are Puruṣas ; Earth and the rest also are multiplied according to the differences of Bodies, jars, etc.

Âśrita, supported : They are supported by their respective causes.

Liṅga, mergent, mark : Buddhi and the rest are marks of the Pradhâna. Gauḍapâda explains the word to mean "subject to dissolution." At the time of the Dissolution the five Great Elements merge into the Tanmâtras, and these together with the eleven Indriyas, into Ahaṃkâra, and this, into Buddhi ; and that merges into the Pradhâna.

Paratantra, subordinate : Buddhi, for instance, when it has to produce its own effect, namely, Ahaṃkâra, has to draw upon Prakṛiti ; otherwise, being weak or exhausted, it will not be able to produce Ahaṃkâra. Similarly, by Ahaṃkâra and the rest also is awaited the inflow of Prakṛiti in the production of their own effects.

24. *Viparîta*, reverse : The Unmanifest is causeless, eternal, all pervading, motion-less, single, self-sustained, the subject of the mark or non-mergent, part-less, and supreme.

The Manifest, the Unmanifest and the Knower contrasted and compared.

त्रिगुणमविवेकि विषयः सामान्यमचेतनं प्रसवधर्मि ।
व्यक्तं तथा प्रधानं तद्विपरीतस्तथा च पुमान् ॥ ११ ॥

त्रिगुणम् Tri-guṇam, having or constituted by the three Guṇas, *viz.*, Sattva, Rajas, and Tamas. अविवेकि A-viveki, non-discriminative. विषयः Viṣayaḥ, objective. सामान्यम् Sâmânyam, common. अचेतनं A-chetanam, non-intelligent. प्रसवधर्मि Prasavadharmi, prolific. व्यक्तं Vyaktam, the Manifest. तथा Tathâ, so. प्रधानं Pradhânam, the Pradhâna, Prakṛiti. तद्विपरीतः Tat-viparîtaḥ, the reverse of this. तथा Tathâ, so. च Cha, yet. पुमान् Pumân, Puruṣa.

XI. The Manifest is constituted by the three Guṇas, is non-discriminative, objective, common, non-intelligent, prolific. So is also the Pradhâna. Puruṣa is the reverse of them both (in these respects), and yet is similar (to the Pradhâna and also to the Manifest in those other respects mentioned in the preceding Kârikâ.)

ANNOTATION.

25. *A-viveki* : Just as the Pradhâna is not discriminated from itself, even so are not Mahat and the rest also discriminated from the Pradhâna, because of their essential identity. Or, A-viveka is to create by uniting

together, for none of them singly are capable of producing their own effects, but, on the contrary, only by uniting together.

Viṣaya: because it is the Object as distinguished from the Subject, to be apprehended and made use of by all Puruṣas alike.

26. *Tathâ cha*, and yet is similar: that is, as the Pradhâna is, in the preceding Kârikâ, declared to be without cause, etc., such is Puruṣa. Thus, "* * * The Manifest is multitudinous; the Unmanifest is single; so is Puruṣa also single.* * *" (Gauḍapâda)." "But when similarity to the Pradhâna belongs to Puruṣa in respect of non-causability, eternality, etc., and likewise multiplicity is his similarity to the Manifest, how is it said that" the reverse of them both is Puruṣa? To this, it is replied: Tathâ cha: Cha has the sense of Api, even, yet; although there is similarity in respect of non-causability, etc., yet he possesses dissimilarity in respect of not being constituted by the three Guṇas, etc. Such is the meaning" (Vâchaspati Miśra). "The S. Chandrikâ confirms the interpretation: 'The phrase *tathâ cha* implies that (soul) is analogous to the undiscrete principle in non-causability and the rest, and analogous to discrete principles in manifold enumeration.' This is, in fact, the Sâṃkhya doctrine, as subsequently laid down by the text, ver. 18, and is conformable to the Sûtra of Kapila; 'Multitude of souls is proved by variety of condition': that is, 'the virtuous are born again in heaven, the wicked are regenerated in hell; the fool wanders in error, the wise man is set free.' Either, therefore, Gauḍapâda has made a mistake, or by his *eka* is to be understood, not that soul in general is one only, but that it is single, or several, in its different migrations; or, as Mr. Colebrooke renders it (R.A.S. Trans. vol. I. p. 31) 'individual.' So in the Sûtras it is said 'that there may be various unions of one soul, according to difference of receptacle, as the etherial element may be confined in a variety of vessels.' This singleness of soul applies therefore to that particular soul which is subjected to its own varied course of birth, death, bondage, and liberation; for, as the commentator observes, 'one soul is born, not another (in a regenerated body)' The singleness of soul, therefore, as asserted by Gauḍapâda, is no doubt to be understood in this sense." (*Wilson*).

Characteristics of the Guṇas described.

प्रीत्यप्रीतिविषादात्मकाः प्रकाशप्रवृत्तिनियमार्थाः ।
अन्योन्याभिभवाश्रयजननमिथुनवृत्तयश्च गुणाः ॥ १२ ॥

प्रीत्यप्रीतिविषादात्मकाः : Prîti-aprîti-visâda-âtmakâh, of the nature of pleasure, pain and dulness. प्रकाशप्रवृत्तिनियमार्थाः : Prakâśa-pravṛitti-niyama-arthâḥ adapted to serving the purpose of, or capable of causing, illumination, activity, and, restraint. अन्योन्याभिभवाश्रयजननमिथुनवृत्तय : Anya-anya-abhibhava-âśraya-janana-mithuna-vrittayaḥ, having mutual domination, dependence, production, consociation, and co-existence. Vâchaspati does not consider the term Vṛitti as a distinct condition; he interprets it as Kriyâ, act, operation or function, and compounds it with each of the foregoing terms. च Cha, and. गुणा : Guṇâḥ, the Guṇas.

XII. The Guṇas possess the nature of pleasure, pain and dulness; serve the purpose of illumination, activity, and restraint; and perform the function of mutual domination, dependence, production, and consociation.

ANNOTATION.

27. Possess the nature, etc: Hereby the intrinsic forms of the Guṇas Sattva, Rajas, and Tamas are declared. The force of the word Âtmâ, nature, is that it is a reply to those who think that pleasure is nothing but absence of pain, and that pain is nothing but absence of pleasure. For Âtmâ denotes being, something positive, and is a negation of non-being.

28. Serve the purpose, etc: Hereby the purposes served by the Guṇas respectively are declared. *Artha* means *prayojana* or purpose. Gauḍapâda interprets the term in the sense of competency, fitness, capability.

29. Perform the functions, etc: Hereby the various operations of the Guṇas are declared.

Dependence: Although dependence, that is, co-existence by the relation of the container and the contained is not possible, still that is the support of that, the operation of which depends upon it. Thus, Sattva, by resting on activity and restraint, subserves Rajas and Tamas with illumination; Rajas, by resting on illumination and restraint, subserves Sattva and Tamas with activity; Tamas, by resting on illumination and activity, subserves Sattva and Rajas with restraint.

Production: Production is transformation, and it is of the same form as the Guṇas; hence causability is not entailed, owing to the absence of a cause which is a different Tattva. Neither is non-eternality entailed, owing to the absence of dissolution into a different Tattva.

Consociation: That is, the Guṇas are constant companions of one another.

Co-existence is explained by Guaḍapâda thus: As a beautiful and amiable woman, who is a source of delight to every one else, is the cause of misery to the other wives of her husband, and of bewilderment to the dissolute; so does Sattva produce the functions of Rajas and Tamas. As a king, assiduous in protecting his people, and curbing the profligate, is the cause of happiness to the good, of misery and mortification to the wicked; so does Rajas produce the functions of Sattva and Tamas. Similarly, Tamas produces the functions of Sattva and Rajas, as clouds, overshadowing the heavens, cause delight upon earth, animate by their rain the active labours of the husbandman, and overwhelm absent lovers with despair. In this manner, the Guṇas perform the functions of one another.

The Co-operation of the Guṇas explained.

सत्त्वं लघु प्रकाशकमिष्टमुपष्टम्भकं चलं च रजः ।
गुरु वरणकमेव तमः प्रदीपवच्चार्थतो वृत्तिः ॥ १३ ॥

सत्त्वं Sattvaṃ, sattva. लघु Laghu, alleviating, light. प्रकाशकम् Prakâśakam, enlightening, illuminating. इष्टम् Iṣṭam, desired, considered. उपष्टम्भकं Upaṣṭambhakaṃ, urgent, exciting. चलं Chalam, versatile, restless. च Cha, and. रजः Rajaḥ, rajas. गुरु Guru, heavy. वरणकम् Varaṇakam enveloping, covering, obscuring. एव Eva, to be sure. तमः Tamaḥ, tamas. प्रदीपवत् Pradîpa-vat, like a lamp. च Cha, and. अर्थतः Artha-taḥ, for a purpose. वृत्तिः Vṛittiḥ, function, operation.

XIII. Sattva is considered to be light and illuminating, and Rajas, to be exciting and restless, and Tamas, to be indeed heavy and enveloping. Like a lamp (consisting of oil, wick, and fire), they co-operate for a (common) purpose (by union of contraries).

ANNOTATION.

30. Contraries need not necessarily oppose and counteract one another. As co-operation of contraries for a common purpose is seen in the case of a lamp, even so is it the case with the Guṇas which co-operate with one another to serve a common purpose, *viz.*, the experience and release of Puruṣa.

31. Granted, one may say, that non-discriminativeness, etc., are proved by perception in the case of Earth, etc., which are objects of perception; but how can Sattva, etc., which are not objects of perception, be said to be non-discriminative, objective, common, non-intelligent, and prolific (Kârikâ XI)? To this, the reply is given in the next Kârikâ.

Proof of the properties of the Unmanifest.

अविवेक्यादेः सिद्धिस्त्रैगुण्यात्तद्विपर्ययाभावात् ।
कारणगुणात्मकत्वात् कार्यस्य अव्यक्तमपि सिद्धम् ॥१४॥

अविवेक्यादेः A-viveki-âdeh, of non-discriminativeness, etc. सिद्धिः Siddhiḥ, proof. त्रैगुण्यात् Traiguṇyât, from their being constituted by the three Guṇas or from their manifesting the three qualities of pleasure, pain, and dulness. तद्विपर्ययाभावात् Tat-viparyaya-abhâvât, from the absence of non-discriminativeness, etc., in the reverse thereof; *i.e.*, of the Manifest and the Unmanifest, *i.e.*, Puruṣa; from the absence of the reverse of Traiguṇya in the Unmanifest; from the absence of the divergence or non-concomitance or disagreement between the properties in question and the Manifest and the Unmanifest or the Unmanifest only. कारणगुणात्मकत्वात् Kâraṇa-guṇa-âtmaka-tvât, from the effect's containing the attributes of the cause. कार्यस्य Kâryasya, of the effect. अव्यक्तम् A-Vyaktam, the Unmanifest. अपि Api, also. सिद्धम् Siddham, proved, established.

XIV. The proof of non-discriminativeness, and the rest (in the Manifest and the Unmanifest) is from their being constituted by the three Guṇas and from absence of their non-concomitance. From the effect possessing the attributes of the cause is proved the Unmanifest also.

ANNOTATION.

32. According to Vâchaspati, the proof of non-discriminativeness and the rest is by the method of agreement, thus;—

Whatever possesses pleasure, pain, and dulness, is non-discriminative, etc.,

As, for instance, are the objects of the senses;

Prakṛiti, Mahat, etc., possess pleasure, pain, and dulness;

They are, therefore, non-discriminative, etc:

and also by the method of difference, thus:—

Whatever is not non-discriminative, etc., does not possess pleasure, pain and dulness,

As, for instance, is the case with Puruṣa.

But Prakṛiti, Mahat, etc., possess pleasure, pain, and dulness;

They are, therefore, not-non-discriminative, etc.

But the proof of these attributes must be subject to the proof of their alleged substratum. How then is this, namely, the Pradhâna proved? Thus: The effect characterised as Mahat, etc., possessing the form of pleasure, pain, and dulness, must have the nature or essence of pleasure, pain, and dulness inhereing in its own cause ; so that its cause, possessing the nature of pleasure, pain, and dulness, that is, the Pradhâna Unmanifest, is established.

33. Gauḍapâda's interpretation is different from the above. According to him, the properties of non-discriminativeness, etc., are proved in the Manifest from their being constituted by the three Guṇas, through the absence of divergence, that is, because the properties of non-discriminativeness, etc., have never been found except in conjunction with the property of being constituted by the three Guṇas. And their existence in the Unmanifest is proved from the absence of divergence, that is, from the invariable and universal concomitance of the Manifest and the Unmanifest : just as, wherever there is the cloth, there are the yarns ; similarly whoever sees the Manifest, sees the Unmanifest as well ; and also from the effect possessing the nature of the cause : thus, from the effect, *viz.*, Mahat and the rest which are non-discriminative, objective, common, non-intelligent, and prolific, is proved that their cause, namely, the Unmanifest, possesses the same properties.

Proof of the Unmanifest.

भेदानां परिमाणात् समन्वयात् शक्तितः प्रवृत्तेश्च ।
कारणकार्यविभागादविभागाद् वैश्वरूपस्य ॥ १५ ॥
कारणमस्त्यव्यक्तं प्रवर्तते त्रिगुणतः समुदयाच्च ।
परिणामतः सलिलवत् प्रतिप्रतिगुणाश्रयविशेषात् ॥१६॥

भेदानां Bhedânâṃ, of differentiated particulars, specific objects, of the evolutes, Mahat and the rest. परिमाणात् Parimâṇât, from finiteness, measurableness. समन्वयात् Samanvayât, from homogeneity, agreement. शक्तितः Sakti-taḥ, from power. प्रवृत्तेः Pravṛitteḥ, from activity, from production. च Cha, and. कारणकार्यविभागात् Kâraṇa-kârya-bibhâgât, from differentiation of cause and effect. अविभागात् A-vibhâgât, from non-differentiation, from reunion. वैश्वरूपस्य Vaiśvarûpasya, of the formal Universe. कारणम् Kâraṇam, cause. अस्ति Asti, exists. अव्यक्तं A-Vyaktam, Unmanifest. प्रवर्तते Pravartate, energises, operates. त्रिगुणतः Tri-guṇa-taḥ, through or of the three Guṇas, Sattva, Rajas, and Tamas. समुदयात् Sam-udayât, through combination, co-operation. च Cha, and. परिणामतः Pariṇâma-taḥ, through transformation. सलिलवत् Salila-vat, like water. प्रतिप्रतिगुणाश्रयविशेषात् Prati-prati-guṇa-âśraya-viśeṣât, through differences according to the differences of the several receptacles of the Guṇas, or differences created by the Guṇas severally based on the principal Guṇa.

XV-XVI. Of the particulars (*e.g.*, Mahat and all the rest down to the earth), there exists an Unmanifest cause :

because the particulars are finite; because they are homogeneous; because production is through power; because there is differentiation of effect from cause or difference of cause and effect; and because there is reunion of the multiform effect with the cause.

It operates, in the form of the three Guṇas and by combination, undergoing transformation, (diversified) according to the differences severally of the other Guṇas depending on the principal Guṇa.

ANNOTATION.

34. Because they are homogeneous: Homogeneousness is the possession of a common form among a number of distinct individuals. The presence of a common form infers a common origin.

Because production is through power: Power inhering in the cause is nothing but the unmanifested state of the effect.

Differentiation and reunion: Discrete products of every sort of form from Mahat down to a jar, for instance, successively rise from their causes at the time of creation and disappear into them at the time of destruction and universal dissolution. The ultimate points in the process of evolution and involution are one and the same. It is the absolute unmanifested state of a single entity. It is called the Unmanifest, the Pradhâna and Prakṛiti.

35. It operates etc.: The Guṇas of which the nature is to undergo transformation, never rest, even for a moment, without transforming themselves. Their transformation may be homogeneous or heterogeneous. Homogeneous transformation takes place during Pralaya or the period of latency intervening Creation and Dissolution, when Sattva transforms as Sattva, Rajas as Rajas, and Tamas as Tamas. Such is the meaning of the phrase Tri-guṇa-taḥ, in the form of the three Guṇas severally. Heterogeneous transformation takes place during Creation and Dissolution. For this, combination of the Guṇas with one another in different proportions is necessary. Such combination is rendered possible by the diversified activity of the Guṇas in the evolution of Mahat and all the rest, of which each successive one is more and more specified than, and differentiated from, its predecessor. And this differentiation is brought about by the difference in the ratio in which the subsidiary Guṇas combine and co-operate with the principal Guṇa. Thus, as regards the eleven Indriyas

and the five Tan-mâtras, while Rajas is equally operative in the evolution of both, the former arise from Ahaṃkâra in which Sattva is predominant and Tamas is dormant; whereas the latter arise from Ahaṃkâra in which Tamas is predominant and Sattva is dormant.

Salila-vat: As simple water shed by the clouds, coming into contact with various situations, is modified as sweet, sour, bitter, pungent, or astringent, in the character of the juice of the cocoa-nut, palm, bel, karanja, amalaka, wood-apple, etc.

Proof of Puruṣa.

संघातपरार्थत्वात् त्रिगुणादिविपर्ययादधिष्ठानात् ।
पुरुषोऽस्ति भोक्तृभावात् कैवल्यार्थं प्रवृत्तेश्च ॥ १७ ॥

संघातपरार्थत्वात् Saṃghâta-para artha-tvât, since an aggregate or structure of manifold parts into one whole is for the sake of another of a different character त्रिगुणादिविपर्ययात् Tri-Guṇa-âdi-viparyayât, since there must exist an entity in which there is the reverse of the properties of being constituted by three Guṇas, and the rest mentioned in Kârikâ XI. अधिष्ठानात् Adhiṣṭhânât, since there must be superintendence over Buddhi and other products of the Guṇas. पुरुषः Puruṣaḥ Puruṣa. अस्ति Asti, exists. भोक्तृभावात् Bhoktṛi-bhâvât, since there must be an experiencer of pleasure and pain. कैवल्यार्थं Kaivalya-arthaṃ, for the sake of isolation. प्रवृत्तेः Pravṛitteḥ, since activity is. च Cha, and.

XVII. Puruṣa exists: since the aggregate must be for the sake of the non-aggregate; since there must exist an entity in which the properties of being constituted by the three Guṇas and the rest do not appear; since there must be a superintendent; since there must be an experiencer; and since activity is for the sake of abstraction.

ANNOTATION.

36. Since there must exist an entity, etc.: Hereby is prevented the inference of an aggregate by the aggregate. For all aggregates possess the three Guṇas, whereas Puruṣa is free from them, as declared in Kârikâ XI. Therefore, the entity for which the aggregate is, must be a non-aggregate. And Puruṣa is a non-aggregate.

Proof of Multiplicity of Puruṣa.

जननमरणकरणानां प्रतिनियमादयुगपत् प्रवृत्तेश्च ।
पुरुषबहुत्वं सिद्धं त्रैगुण्यविपर्ययाच्चैव ॥ १८ ॥

जननमरणकरणानां Janana-maraṇa-karaṇânâṃ, of birth, death, and the instrument of cognition and action. प्रतिनियमात् Prati-niyamât, individual allotment. अयुगपत्

A-yugapat, non-simultaneous. प्रवृत्तेः Pravṛitteḥ, from activity or occupation. च Cha, and. पुरुषबहुत्वं Puruṣa-bahu-tvaṃ, multiplicity of Puruṣas. सिद्धं Siddhaṃ, established. त्रैगुण्यविपर्ययात् Traiguṇya-viparyayât, from absence of the condition of the three Guṇas, from diverse modification of the three Guṇas. च Cha, and. एव Eva, verily.

XVIII. From the individual allotment of birth, death and the Instruments, from non-simultaneous activity (towards the same end), and from the diverse modification of the three Guṇas, multitude of Puruṣas is verily established.

ANNOTATION.

37. Birth consists in conjunction with body, Indriya, Manas, Ahaṃkâra, Buddhi, and experience, and death consists in their abandonment. So that they do not entail the transformation of Puruṣa. The distribution of body and the rest, which is different in each individual case, must imply a plurality of Puruṣas, as, otherwise, on the birth of one, all would be born and on the death of one, all would die.

Non-simultaneous activity towards the same end: as, *e.g.*, some are busy with virtuous, others with vicious, actions; some cultivate dispassion, others knowledge.

Diverse modification of the three Guṇas: thus, though birth is common to all, one possessing Sattva is happy, another possessing Rajas, is wretched, and a third possessing Tamas, is dull.

Proof of the Nature of Puruṣa.

तस्माच्च विपर्यासात् सिद्धं साक्षित्वमस्य पुरुषस्य ।
कैवल्यं माध्यस्थ्यं द्रष्टृत्वमकर्तृभावश्च ॥ १९ ॥

तस्मात् Tasmât, from that. च Cha, and. विपर्यासात् Viparyâsât, from contrast, divergence. सिद्धं Siddhaṃ, proved. साक्षित्वं Sâkṣi-tvaṃ, to be the witness. अस्य Asya, of this. पुरुषस्य Puruṣa-sya, of Puruṣa. कैवल्यं Kaivalyaṃ, aloneness, solitariness. माध्यस्थ्यं Mâdhyasthyaṃ, indifference, to be the bystander. द्रष्टृत्वम् Draṣṭri-tvaṃ, to be the spectator. अकर्तृभावः A-kartri-bhâvaḥ, non-agent-ship. च Cha, and.

XIX. And from that contrast it is proved that this Puruṣa is witness, solitary, indifferent, spectator, and non-agent.

ANNOTATION.

38. That contrast: that is, Puruṣa is not constituted by the three Guṇas, is discriminative, is not objective but subjective, is not common, is intelligent, and is not prolific (see Kârikâ XIV).

Because he is intelligent and subjective, he is spectator and witness. A witness is one to whom objects are shown. Prakṛiti exhibits herself to Puruṣa.

From his not being constituted by the three Guṇas follow his solitariness and indifference. For solitariness consists in the absolute non-existence of the three sorts of pain, and indifference denotes absence of love for pleasure and hate for pain. But pleasure and pain are properties of the three Guṇas. And because Puruṣa is not constituted by the three Guṇas, he is absolutely free from pleasure, pain and bewilderment.

And since he is discriminative and non-prolific, he is not the agent.

But if Puruṣa is a non-agent, how does he make determination? as I will perform acts of merit, I will not perform acts of demerit: hence Puruṣa must be the agent; neither is Puruṣa the agent;—thus there is, may say our opponent, defect in both the theories. Accordingly, the seeming agency of Puruṣa is explained in the next Kârikâ.

The agency of Puruṣa is not real, but fictitious.

तस्मात्तत्संयोगादचेतनं चेतनावदिव लिङ्गम् ।
गुणकर्तृत्वे च तथा कर्तेव भवत्युदासीनः ॥ २० ॥

तस्मात् Tasmât, therefore. तत्संयोगात् Tat-saṃyogât, from conjunction therewith, *i.e.*, with the intelligent Puruṣa. अचेतनं A-chetanam, the non-intelligent. चेतनावत् Chetanâ-vat, possessing intelligence. इव Iva, like, as if. लिङ्गम् Liṅgam, the effect, Mahat and the rest. गुणकर्तृत्वे Guṇa-kartṛi-tve, in the case of the agency of the Guṇas. च Cha, and. तथा Tathâ, likewise. कर्ता Kartâ, agent. इव Iva, like, as if. भवति Bhavati, becomes. उदासीनः Udâsînaḥ, indifferent, *i.e.*, Puruṣa.

XX. Therefore (the inference that intelligence and agency belong to one and the same subject is a mistake.) Through conjunction with Puruṣa, the non-intelligent Effect appears as if it were intelligent, and although agency is of the Guṇas, the indifferent (Puruṣa) appears, in the same way, as if he were the agent.

39. Liṅgam here denotes Mahat, Ahaṃkâra, Manas and the five Tan-mâtras. See Kârikâ XL.

40. The confusion then is due to the conjunction of Prakṛiti and Puruṣa. And conjunction means mutual approach and co-operation,

which necessarily pre-supposes some object or purpose to be achieved. That purpose can be nothing but mutual benefit, as declared in the following Kârikâ.

Object of the conjunction of Puruṣa and Prakṛiti.

पुरुषस्य दर्शनार्थं कैवल्यार्थं तथा प्रधानस्य ।
पङ्ग्वन्धवदुभयोरपि संयोगस्तत्कृतः सर्गः ॥२१॥

पुरुषस्य Puruṣa-sya, of Puruṣa. दर्शनार्थं Darśana-artham, for the sake of seeing or exhibition. कैवल्यार्थं Kaivalya-artham, for the sake of separation. तथा Tathâ, likewise. प्रधानस्य Pradhâna-sya, of the Pradhâna. पङ्ग्वन्धवत् Paṅgu-andha-vat, like that of the halt and the blind. उभयोः Ubhayoḥ, of both. अपि Api, also. संयोगः Saṃyogaḥ, conjunction. तत्कृतः Tat-kritaḥ, originated by that, *i.e.*, conjunction. सर्गः Sargaḥ, creation, evolution.

XXI. The conjunction of Puruṣa and the Pradhâna is, like that of the halt and the blind, for mutual benefit, that is, for the exhibition of the Pradhâna to Puruṣa and for the isolation of Puruṣa. From this conjunction proceeds Creation.

ANNOTATION.

41. The halt and the blind: "As a lame man and a blind man, deserted by their fellow-travellers, who, in making their way with difficulty through a forest, had been dispersed by robbers, happening to encounter each other, and entering into conversation so as to inspire mutual confidence, agreed to divide between them the duties of walking and of seeing; accordingly the lame man was mounted on the blind man's shoulders, and was thus carried on his journey, whilst the blind man was enabled to pursue his route by the directions of his companion. In the same manner, the faculty of seeing is in soul, not that of moving; it is like the lame man: the faculty of moving, but not of seeing, is in nature; which resembles, therefore, the blind man. Further, as a separation takes place between the lame man and the blind man, when their mutual object is accomplished, and they have reached their journey's end, so nature, having effected the liberation of soul, ceases to act; and soul, having contemplated nature, obtains abstractedness; and, consequently, their respective purposes being effected, the connexion between them is dissolved."—Gauḍapâda's Bhâṣya, translated by Wilson.

The Evolutions of Prakṛiti and the order of their evolution stated.

प्रकृतेर्महांस्ततोऽहंकारस्तस्माद्गणश्च षोडशकः ।
तस्मादपि षोडशकात् पञ्चभ्यः पञ्च भूतानि ॥ २२ ॥

प्रकृते: Prakṛiteḥ, from Prakṛiti. महान् Mahân, Mahat. ततः Tataḥ, thence, from Mahat. अहंकारः Ahaṃkâraḥ, Ahaṃkâra. तस्मात् Tasmât, therefrom, from Ahaṃkâra. गणः Gaṇaḥ, set, group, series. च Cha, and. षोडशकः Ṣoḍaśakaḥ, sixteenfold. तस्मात् Tasmât, from that. अपि Api, again. षोडशकात् Ṣoḍaśakât, from sixteenfold. पञ्चभ्यः Pañcha-bhyaḥ, from the five. पञ्च भूतानि Pañcha bhûtâni, the five gross elements.

XXII. From Prakṛiti (evolves) Mahat; thence, Ahaṃkâra ; and from this, the sixteenfold set ; from five, again, among the sixteenfold, the five Elements.

ANNOTATION.

42. The sixteenfold set : that is, the eleven Indriyas and the five Tan-mâtras. From five, etc : that is, from the lower five among the sixteen, that is, the five Tan-mâtras.

Five Elements : *viz.*, Ether, Air, Fire, Water and Earth.

43. The synonyms of Prakṛiti are Pradhâna, that in which all things are contained, Brahmâ, that which expands, A-vyakta, the unmanifest, Bahu-dhânaka, that in which manifold things are contained, Mâyâ, that which measures or limits.

The synonyms of Mahat are Buddhi, that which makes things known, Âsurî, probably Chheda-bheda-âdi-âtmikâ as in the medical science, that is, that which causes separation, differentiation, etc., Mati, that by which things are understood, Khyâti, that by which things are manifested, Jñâna, that by which knowledge is acquired, Prajñâ, that by which perfect knowledge is obtained.

The synonyms of Ahaṃkâra are Bhûta-âdi, the origin of the Bhûtas or elements, Vaikṛita, the modified, Taijasa, partaking of Tejas, *i.e.*, Rajas, Abhimâna, self-consciousness.

By Tattva is meant the Tva, *i.e.*, condition or existence of Tat, or that by which all the three worlds are pervaded. Prakṛiti, Mahat, Ahaṃkâra, Manas, the Indriyas, the Tan-mâtras and the Elements are then the physical and metaphysical existences, realities, or principles pervading all the three worlds.

Buddhi and its modifications described.

अध्यवसायो बुद्धिर्धर्मो ज्ञानं विराग ऐश्वर्यम् ।
सात्त्विकमेतद्रूपं तामसमस्माद्विपर्यस्तम् ॥ २३ ॥

अध्यवसायः Adhyavasâyaḥ, ascertainment. बुद्धिः Buddhiḥ, Mahat, Buddhi. धर्मः Dharmaḥ, virtue, merit. ज्ञानं Jñânam, knowledge. विरागः Virâgaḥ, dispassion. ऐश्वर्यम् Aiśvaryam, lordliness, power. सात्त्विकम् Sâttvikam, partaking of Sattva. एतद्रूपं Etata-rupam, its forms. तामसम् Tâmasam, partaking of Tamas. अस्मात् Asmât, from this. विपर्यस्तम् Viparyastam, the reverse.

XXIIII. Ascertainment is Buddhi. Virtue, knowledge, dispassion and power are its forms or manifestations or modifications, partaking of Sattva. Those partaking of Tamas, are the reverse of these.

ANNOTATION.

44. Ascertainment is Buddhi: this statement in apposition is intended to teach that there is no difference between the function and the fuctionary.

Ascertainment is to arrive at the certainty that this is a jar, this I will do, etc., which is above the stage of doubt, differentiation, assimilation, and deliberation.

Virtue is that which is the cause of happiness and release, and includes the fruits of sacrifices and of the practice of Yoga as taught by Patañjali.

Knowledge is the manfestation of the discrimination between Prakṛiti and Puruṣa.

Dispassion is absence of Râga or passion. It has four names: the name of Yatamâna, Vyatireka, Ekendriya and Vaśîkâra. Passion and the like, which act like dyes of different hues, reside in the Chitta or the Retentive Faculty. By them the Indriyas, the Powers of Cognition and Action, are employed on their respective objects. Now, the endevour, *i.e.*, the putting forth of energy for the purpose of boiling down and dissolving them, with the desire that the Indriyas may not go out to the objects, is designated as Yatamâna. And when the boiling is once begun, some passions will become boiled, while others will be in the course of being boiled. In that stage, the relation of before and after thus coming into existence, the ascertainment of the boiled by means of their discrimination from those that are in the course of being boiled, is designated as Vyatireka. They being thus disabled to excite the Indriyas to activity, the persistence of the boiled passions in the mind in the form of mere longing, is designated as Ekendriya The surcease of even the mere longing in regard to sensible and scriptural objects of enjoyment, even though they be near at hand, which, in its appearance, is subsequent to the first three stages, is designated as Vaśîkâra.—Vâchaspati.

Power is will-power or thought-power, whereby a Yogin becomes at will light as a leaf or heavy as a hill, whereby he can ascend to the sun on a sunbeam or can touch the moon with the tip of his finger, etc.

Partaking of Sattva : that is, when Sattva becomes predominant in Buddhi, by subduing Rajas and Tamas.

Partaking of Tamas : that is, when Tamas becomes predominant in Buddhi, by subduing Sattva and Rajas.

The reverse are vice, ignorance, passion and weakness.

Ahaṃkâra and its Modifications described.

अभिमानोऽहंकारस्तस्मात् द्विविधः प्रवर्तते सर्गः ।
एकादशकश्च गणस्तन्मात्रपञ्चकश्चैव ॥ २४ ॥

अभिमानः Abhimânaḥ, consciousness, self-assertion. अहंकारः Ahaṃkâraḥ, Ahaṃkâra. तस्मात् Tasmât, from it. द्विविधः Dvi-vidhaḥ, twofold. प्रवर्तते Pravartate, proceeds. सर्गः Sargaḥ, creation, evolution. एकादशकः Ekâdaśakaḥ, elevenfold. च Cha, and. गणः Gaṇaḥ, set, series. तन्मात्रपञ्चकं Tan-mâtra-pañchakam, the pentad of the Tan-mâtras. च Cha, and. एव Eva, nothing else.

XXIV. Self-assertion is Ahaṃkâra. From it proceeds a twofold evolution only : the elevenfold set and also the fivefold Tan-mâtra.

ANNOTATION.

45. The elevenfold set comprises the eleven Indriyas, *i.e.*, the five Indriyas of cognition and the five Indriyas of action and Manas.

The fivefold Tan-mâtra comprises the subtile particles or essences which are Sound, Touch, Form, Taste, and Smell. Whatever word conveys the sense of subtilty or fineness is a synonym of Tan-mâtra.

Self-assertion : All that is considered (âlochita) and reasoned (mata) refers to me, in this I am competent, all these objects of sense are for my sake only, this does not concern any one else but me, hence I am,—such abhimâna, self-assertion or consciousness by reference to oneself, from its having an uncommon or unique operation of its own, is called Ahaṃkâra, by working upon which Buddhi determines that this is to be done by me.

Transformations of Ahaṃkâra distinguished.

सात्त्विक एकादशकः प्रवर्तते वैकृतादहंकारात् ।
भूतादेस्तन्मात्रः स तामसस्तैजसादुभयम् ॥ २५ ॥

सात्त्विकः Sâttvikaḥ, partaking of Sattva, in which Sattva is dominant, pure. एकादशकः Ekâdaśakaḥ, elevenfold. प्रवर्तते Pravartate, proceeds. वैकृतात् vaikṛitât, modified by the predominance of Sattva ; an older term conveying the same sense as Sâttvika. अहंकारात् Ahaṃkârât, from Ahamkâra. भूतादेः Bhûta-âdeḥ, from the original of the elements in which Tamas is dominant ; an older term conveying the same sense as Tâmasa. तन्मात्रः Tan-mâtraḥ, the Tan-mâtras. सः Saḥ, it. तामसः Tâmasaḥ, Tâmasa, having Tamas dominant in it. तैजसात् Taijasât, from Taijasa, which is an older term having the sense of Râjasa, that in which Rajas is dominant. उभयम् Ubhayam, both, *i.e.*, the Indriyas and the Tan-mâtras.

XXV. The Sâttvika elevenfold set proceeds from the Vaikṛita Ahaṃkâra ; from the Bhûtâdi Ahaṃkâra, the Tan-mâtras ; they are Tâmasa ; from Taijasa-Ahaṃkâra, proceed both.

ANNOTATION.

46. From the Taijasa, both : Of the three Guṇas, Rajas alone is exciting and restless (see Kârikâ XIII). Rajas alone, therefore, is active while Sattva and Tamas are inert. These must then depend upon the activity of Rajas for the evolution of their products. It is in this sense that from the Taijasa proceed both, and not that a duplicate set of the Indriyas and the Tan-mâtras simultaneously issue from the Râjasa Ahaṃkâra.

Indriyas enumerated.

बुद्धीन्द्रियाणि चक्षुःश्रोत्रघ्राणरसनत्वगाख्यानि ।
वाक्पाणिपादपायूपस्थान् कर्मेन्द्रियाण्याहुः ॥ २६ ॥

बुद्धीन्द्रियाणि Bûddhi-indriyâṇi, the Indriyas or Powers of cognition. चक्षुःश्रोत्रघ्राणरसनत्वगाख्यानि Chakṣuḥ-śrotra-ghrâṇa-rasana-tvak-âkhyâni, called the eyes, ears, nose, tongue, and skin. वाक्पाणिपादपायूपस्थान् Vâk-pâṇi-pâda-pâyu-upasthân, speech, hands, feet, excretory organ and organ of generation. कर्मेन्द्रियाणि Karma-indriyâṇi, the Indriyas or Powers of action. आहुः Âhuḥ, they say.

XXVI. Those called the eyes, the ears, the nose, the tongue and the skin are said to be the Indriyas of cognition, and the speech, hands, feet, the excretory organ and the organ of generation, to be the Indriyas of action.

Manas described.

उभयात्मकमत्र मनः संकल्पकमिन्द्रियञ्च साधर्म्यात् ।
गुणपरिणामविशेषान्नानात्वं बाह्यभेदाश्च ॥ २७ ॥

उभयात्मकम् Ubhaya-âtmakam, possessing the nature of both, *i.e.* Indriyas of cognition and of action. अत्र Atra, herein, in the set of Indriyas. मनः Manaḥ, Manas. संकल्पकम् Saṃkalpakam, that which forms a complete idea at last, by means of assimilation and differenitation ; reflective ; deliberative ; combinative. इन्द्रियं Indriyaṃ, indriya. च Cha, as well. साधर्म्यात् Sâdharmyât, from homogeneousness. गुणपरिणामविशेषात् Guṇa-pariṇâma-viseṣât, from differences in the transformation of the Guṇas. नानात्वं Nânâ-tvaṃ, manifoldness ; variety ; diverseness. बाह्यभेदाः Bâhya-bhedâḥ, external diversities. च Cha, and.

XXVII. Among the Indriyas, Manas possesses the nature of both. It is deliberative, and is as well an Indriya, as it is homogeneous with the rest. The variety of the Indriyas is due to the differences in the transformation of the Guṇas, and so are the external diversities (of objects of the senses).

ANNOTATION.

47. Nature of both : The presence of Manas is necessary both in respect to cognition and in respect to action ; for, to quote from Locke, "a man whose mind is intently employed in the contemplation of some objects, takes no notice of impressions made by sounding bodies upon the organ of hearing : therefore it is evident that perception is only when the mind receives the impression." Similarly, there can be no movement of the hands, etc., without the co-operation of Manas.

48. Saṃkalpa or deliberation is the uncommon or distinctive function of Manas. By the form of deliberation, Manas is marked out, because, when a thing is first simply observed by the sense as It is something, and doubt arises as to whether it be this or whether it be that, Manas perfectly images it as It is this and not that, that is to say, discriminates the thing as a particular substance possessing specific attributes. In other words, from the materials of the senses, Manas creates percepts. These are then transferred to Ahaṃkâra, which regards them either as concerning itself or not concerning itself. Thus coloured with the personal equation, they are next taken up by Buddhi, which makes certain their true nature and determines conduct accordingly. Such, in brief, is the process of sensuous cognition propounded in the Sâmkhya Darśana.

4

49. But Manas thus possesses a unique definition of its own, yet it does not lie altogether out of the category of the Indriyas, like Buddhi and Ahaṃkâra; for, unlike them, it is, along with the other Indriyas, produced from the same material cause, *viz.*, Ahaṃkâra modified by the predominance of Sattva. Hence, Manas also is an Indriya.

50. But how, from the same material, are diverse effects, *viz.*, eleven Indriyas of eleven sorts, produced? Further, the eleven Indriyas necessarily imply, and must depend for their existence upon, eleven different sorts of objects. How is this diversity created? when the Pradhâna, Buddhi, and Ahaṃkâra are non-intelligent, and Puruṣa is a non-agent. Is it created by Îśvara or by Svabhâva or Spontaneity? The answer is, that a certain Spontaneity is the cause of the variety of the Indriyas and their objects. Just as through Spontaneity, secretion of milk takes place for the growth of the calf, so the Guṇas become spontaneously modified by the forms of the eleven Indriyas for the benefit of Puruṣa. Similarly, through particular transformation of the Guṇas spontaneously, external objects of various kinds are produced; for whatever is the modification of the Guṇas, is their object; hence, external objects must be understood to be the products of the Guṇas.

"Vâchaspati understands the allusion to external objects to be merely illustrative; that is, the internal organs are diversified by the modification of the qualities, in the same manner that external objects are varied by the same modification".—Wilson's free translation.

Vijñâna Bhikṣu reads the passage as Bâhya-bhedât cha, and from the variety of external objects, instead of Bâhya-bhedâḥ cha, and so are the external diversities.

The Functions of the Indriyas described.

शब्दादिषु पञ्चानामालोचनमात्रमिष्यते वृत्तिः ।
वचनादानविहरणोत्सर्गानन्दाश्च पञ्चानाम् ॥ २८ ॥

शब्दादिषु Śabda-âdi-ṣu, in respect to sound and the rest, *i.e.*, form, touch, taste, and smell. पञ्चानां Pañchânâm, of the five, *i.e.*, senses of cognition. आलोचनमात्रम् Âlochana-mâtram, observation simply, the mere observation of things, the identity of which is not free from doubt. इष्यते Iṣyate, is considered. वृत्तिः Vṛittiḥ, modification,. function. वचनादानविहरणोत्सर्गानन्दाः Vachana-âdâna-viharaṇa-utsarga-ânandâḥ, speech, manipulation, locomotion, excretion and generation. च Cha, and. पञ्चानाम् Pñchânâm, of the five, Indriyas of action.

XXVIII. The function of the five, in respect to sound and the rest, is considered to be observation simply. Speech, manipulation, locomotion, excretion and generation are considered to be the functions of the other five.

The common and uncommon functions of the Antaḥ-Karaṇas distinguished.

स्वालक्षण्यं वृत्तिस्त्रयस्य सैषा भवत्यसामान्या ।
सामान्यकरणवृत्तिः प्राणाद्या वायवः पञ्च ॥ २९ ॥

स्वालक्षण्यं Svâlakṣaṇyam, the condition of having specific or distinctive or uncommon or characteristic definitions of their own. वृत्तिः Vṛittiḥ, function, operation. त्रयस्य Traya-sya, of the three, *viz.*, Buddhi, Ahaṃkâra, and Manas. सा Sâ, the same. एषा Eṣâ, this. भवति Bhavati, is. असामान्या A-sâmânyâ, uncommon, peculiar to each. सामान्यकरणवृत्तिः Sâmânaya-karaṇa-vṛittiḥ the common function or modification of the Instruments. प्राणाद्याः Prâṇa-âdyâḥ, Prâṇa and the rest, *viz.*, Apâna, Samâna, Udâna, and Vyâna, the five vital airs, life-breaths. वायवः Vâyavaḥ, airs. पञ्च Pañcha, five.

XXIX. Of the three (internal Instruments), their own definitions are their respective functions. These, the same, (functions) are peculiar to each. The common modification of the Instruments is the five airs beginning with Prâṇa.

ANNOTATION.

51. It is to be noted that the five vital airs are taught to be the modifications jointly of Buddhi, Ahaṃkâra, and Manas, and not of the elements, as otherwise might be imagined.

The functions of the Indriyas are successive as well as simultaneous.

युगपच्चतुष्टयस्य तु वृत्तिः क्रमशश्च तस्य निर्दिष्टा ।
दृष्टे तथाप्यदृष्टे त्रयस्य तत्पूर्विका वृत्तिः ॥ ३० ॥

युगपत् Yugapat, simultaneous, consentaneous. चतुष्टयस्य Chatuṣṭayasya, of the quartet, *viz.*, Buddhi, Ahaṃkâra, Manas, and one of the external senses. तु Tu, but. वृत्तिः Vṛittiḥ, function. क्रमशः Krama-śaḥ, successively, gradually. च Cha, and. तस्य Tasya, its, of the quartet. निर्दिष्टा Nirdiṣṭâ, found. दृष्टे Driṣṭe, in the case of the seen, in regard to sensible objects, in the case of perceptual cognition. तथापि Tathâ api, so too. अदृष्टे A-driṣṭe, in regard to supra-sensible objects, in the case of the unseen, in the case of cognition by inference, testimony, revelation, and recollection. त्रयस्य Traya-sya, of the triad, *viz.*, Buddhi, Ahaṃkâra, and Manas. तत्पूर्विका Tat-pûrvikâ, preceded by that, the seen. वृत्तिः Vṛittiḥ, function.

XXX. Of all the four, the functions are instantaneous; their functions are found to be successive also. This is in regard to sensible objects. In regard to unseen objects, so too are the functions of the three, but preceded by that.

ANNOTATION.

52. Instantaneous: as when one suddenly comes across a tiger in a dark night, one's eyes at once observe, Manas considers, Ahaṃkâra identifies, and Buddhi determines, and the man immediately runs away for his life.

Successive: as when a man sees in dim light something moving in front of him and doubt arises as to what it might be; his Manas considers that it is nothing but a robber; his Ahaṃkâra makes him self-conscious that he is approaching towards him; and his Buddhi determines, I must move away.

So too: that is, in the case of non-perceptual cognition, the functions of Buddhi, Ahaṃkâra, and Manas may be simultaneous as well as successive.

But preceded by that: Hereby the condition of cognition by inference, revelation, and recollection is laid down, which may be stated in the phraseology of Locke as that nothing can be in the intellect which was not previously in the senses. For there can be no inference or revelation or recollection of what has never before been perceived.

How the Indriyas act in harmony with one another.

स्वां स्वां प्रतिपद्यन्ते परस्पराकूतहेतुकां वृत्तिम् ।
पुरुषार्थ एव हेतुर्न केनचित् कार्यते करणम् ॥ ३१ ॥

स्वां स्वां Svâṃ svâṃ, own, own. प्रतिपद्यन्ते Pratipadyante, reach, enter into. परस्पराकूतहेतुकां Paraspara-âkûta-hetukâṃ, of which the cause is proneness to activity arising from mutual sympathy. वृत्तिम् Vṛittim, function, modification. पुरुषार्थः Puruṣa-arthaḥ, the purpose of Puruṣa. एव Eva, alone. हेतुः Hetuḥ, cause, motive. न Na, not. केनचित् Kena chit, by any one whatever. कार्यते Kâryate, wrought, made to act. करणम् Karaṇaṃ, instrument.

XXXI. The Instruments enter into their respective modifications to which they are incited by mutual desire. The purpose of Puruṣa is the only (cause of the activity of the Instruments). By none whatever is an Instrument made to act.

The number, functions and effects of the Indriyas described.

करणं त्रयोदशविधं तदाहरणधारणप्रकाशकरम् ।
कार्यञ्च तस्य दशधाहार्यं धार्यं प्रकाश्यञ्च ॥ ३२ ॥

करणं Karaṇam, instrument. त्रयोदशविधं Trayodaśa-vidhaṃ, thirteenfold. तत् Tat, it. आहरणधारणप्रकाशकरं Âharaṇa-dhâraṇa-prakâśa-karam, performer of apprehension, sustentation and manifestation. कार्यं Kâryaṃ, effect. च Cha, and. तस्य Tasya, its. दशधा Daśa-dhâ, tenfold. आहार्यं Âhâryaṃ, apprehensible. धार्यं Dhâryaṃ, sustainable. प्रकाश्यं Prakâśyaṃ, manifestable. च Cha, and.

XXXII. The Instrument is of thirteen sorts. It performs apprehension, sustentation, and manifestation. And its effect or act, *viz.*, the apprehensible, the sustainable, and the manifestable, is (each) tenfold.

ANNOTATION.

53. Apprehension is of the five instruments of action. Their effects are speech, manipulation, locomotion, excretion and generation, which being distinguished as earthly and non-earthly, become tenfold.

Sustentation is of the five vital airs, which support the Body. The thing to be sustained, *i.e.*, Body, is fivefold according as it is made of Earth, Water, Fire, Air, and Ether, and these, again, being distinguished as celestial (divya) and non-celestial, become tenfold.

Manifestation is of the five instruments of cognition. The things to be manifested are sound, touch, form, taste, and smell, and these being distinguished as celestial and non-celestial, become tenfold.

Gauḍapâda explains the Kârikâ differently. According to him, the instruments of action apprehend and sustain, those of cognition manifest. The action or effect of these instruments is tenfold, *viz.*, sound, etc., and speech, etc. Thus, what is manifested by the instruments of cognition, is acquired and maintained by those of action.

The Thirteen Indriyas described and distinguished.

अन्तःकरणं त्रिविधं दशधा बाह्यं त्रयस्य विषयाख्यम् ।
साम्प्रतकालं बाह्यं त्रिकालमाभ्यन्तरं करणम् ॥ ३३ ॥

अन्तःकरणं Antaḥ-Karaṇaṃ, the internal instrument. त्रिविधं Tri-vidhaṃ, threefold. दशधा Daśa-dhâ, tenfold. बाह्यं Bâhyaṃ, external. त्रयस्य Trayasya, of the three. विषयाख्यम् Viṣaya-âkhyam, called object. साम्प्रतकालं Sâmprata-kâlaṃ, at time present. बाह्यं Bâhyaṃ, external. त्रिकालम् Tri-kâlam, at three times, *i.e.*, time past, present and future. आभ्यन्तरं Âbhyantaraṃ, internal. करणम् Karaṇam, instrumen.

XXXIII. The internal Instrument is threefold; the external, tenfold, called the object of the three. The external instrument operates at time present; the internal at all the three times.

ANNOTATION.

54. Called the object of the three: because the external instruments of cognition and action are the channels through which the three internal instruments of Buddhi, Ahaṃkâra, and Manas come into contact with, and exercise their functions in regard to, the external objects.

Objects of the Indriyas described.

बुद्धीन्द्रियाणि तेषां पञ्च विशेषाविशेषविषयाणि ।
वागभवति शब्दविषया शेषाणि तु पञ्चविषयाणि ॥३४॥

बुद्धीन्द्रियाणि Buddhi-indriyâṇi, the Indriyas of cognition. तेषां Teṣâṃ, of these. पञ्च Pañcha, five. विशेषाविशेषविषयाणि Viśeṣa-aviśeṣa-viṣayâṇi, having as their objects gross sound, etc., causing pleasure, pain, and dulness, and subtile sound, etc., in the form of the Tan-mâtras. वाक Vâk, speech. भवति Bhavati, is. शब्दविषया Śabda-viṣayâ, having sound as object. शेषाणि Śeṣâṇi, the rest, i.e., hands, feet, the excretory organ and the organ of generation. तु Tu, but. पञ्चविषयाणि Pañcha-viṣayâṇi, having all the five, sound, etc., as objects.

XXXIV. Among these (ten Indriyas) the five Indriyas of cognition have for their objects things gross and subtile. Speech has sound (alone) for its object. But the rest have (all) the five as their objects.

ANNOTATION.

55. But the rest have the five etc.: for, a jar, *e.g.*, which may be taken hold of by the hand, possesses sound, touch, form, taste, and smell; the foot treads upon the earth of which sound and the rest are the characteristics; the excretory organ separates that in which these five abide; and the organ of generation produces the secretion in which all these five are present.

Why Buddhi is principal among the Indriyas.

सान्तःकरणा बुद्धिः सर्वं विषयमवगाहते यस्मात् ।
तस्मात्त्रिविधं करणं द्वारि द्वाराणि शेषाणि ॥ ३५ ॥

सान्तःकरणा Sa-antaḥ-karaṇâ, together with the internal instruments of Ahaṃkâra and Manas. बुद्धिः Buddhiḥ, Buddhi. सर्वं Sarvaṃ, all. विषयम् Viṣayam, object. अवगाहते Avagâhate, adverts to, comprehends. यस्मात् Yasmât, since. तस्मात् Tasmât, therefore. त्रिविधं Tri-vidhaṃ, threefold. करणं Karaṇaṃ, instrument. द्वारि Dvâri, warders, gatemen, room. द्वाराणि Dvârâṇi, gates. शेषाणि Seṣâṇi, rest.

XXXV. Since Buddhi, together with Ahaṃkâra and Manas, comprehends all objects (at all times), therefore, the three Instruments are like a house of which the rest are gates.

Above continued.

एते प्रदीपकल्पाः परस्परविलक्षणा गुणविशेषाः ।
कृत्स्नं पुरुषस्यार्थं प्रकाश्य बुद्धौ प्रयच्छंति ॥ ३६ ॥

एते Ete, these, the ten external Indriyas, Manas, and Ahaṃkâra. प्रदीपकल्पाः Pradîpa-kalpâḥ, comparable to a lamp. परस्परविलक्षणाः Paraspara-vilakṣaṇâḥ, characteristically different from one another. गुणविशेषाः Guṇa-viśeṣâḥ, particular modifications of the Guṇas. कृत्स्नं Kṛitsnaṃ, whole. पुरुषस्य Puruṣa-sya, of, *i.e.*, to Puruṣa. अर्थं Arthaṃ, object. प्रकाश्य Prakâśya, manifesting. बुद्धौ Buddhau, to Buddhi. प्रयच्छंति Prayachchhanti, present, make over.

XXXVI. These particular modifications of the Guṇas, which are characteristically different from one another, and which are, therefore, in this matter, comparable to a lamp, present all their respective objects to Buddhi, so that these may be exhibited to Puruṣa.

ANNOTATION.

56. Comparable to a lamp : see Kârikâ XIII.

Present......to Buddhi : for Puruṣa can experience objects, pleasure, etc., only such as are lodged in Buddhi. The process by which ideas are conveyed to Puruṣa is here described.

Above continued.

सर्वं प्रत्युपभोगं यस्मात् पुरुषस्य साधयति बुद्धिः ।
सैव च विशिनष्टि पुनः प्रधानपुरुषान्तरं सूक्ष्मम् ॥ ३७॥

सर्वं Sarvaṃ, all. प्रति Prati, in regard to. उपभोगं Upa-Bhogaṃ, experience through conjunction. यस्मात् Yasmât, since. पुरुषस्य Puruṣa-sya, of Puruṣa. साधयति Sâdhayati, effects, accomplishes. बुद्धिः Buddhiḥ, Buddhi. सा Sâ, it. एव Eva, the same. च Cha, and. विशिनष्टि Viśinaṣṭi, differentiates, discriminates. पुनः Punaḥ, again. प्रधानपुरुषान्तरं Pradhâna-puruṣa-antaram, difference between the Pradhâna and Puruṣa. सूक्ष्मम् Sukṣaṃ subtile, difficult to discern, not to be apprehended by those who have not practised religious austerities.

XXXVII. (The other Indriyas present all objects to Buddhi, so that they may be exhibited to Puruṣa), since it is Buddhi which accomplishes the experience of Puruṣa in regard to all (objects at all times). And it is that, again, which discriminates the subtile difference between the Pradhâna and Puruṣa.

ANNOTATION.

57. In these three Kârikâs it is established that Buddhi is supreme among the Indriyas. It is the principal means of accomplishing the apparently contradictory purposes of Puruṣa, *viz.*, experience and release. For Buddhi, through the adjacence of Puruṣa, by means of the falling of his shadow, becoming verily of his form, accomplishes Puruṣa's experience of all objects; for experience consists in the apprehension of pleasure and pain, and this exists in Buddhi, and Buddhi is verily of the form of Puruṣa; hence it causes experience to Puruṣa. And while, on the one hand, it is the cause of experience, it is, on the other hand, the cause of release as well, since it is Buddhi which causes discrimination between Prakṛiti and Puruṣa.

The Tan-mâtras and their products described.

तन्मात्राण्यविशेषास्तेभ्यो भूतानि पञ्च पञ्चभ्यः ।
एते स्मृता विशेषाः शान्ता घोराश्च मूढाश्च ॥ ३८ ॥

तन्मात्राणि Tan-mâtrâṇi, Tan-mâtras, subtile elements, the originals of atoms. अविशेषाः A-viśeṣâḥ, indistinguishables, indiscernibles, undifferentiated as pleasant, painful or dull. तेभ्यः Tebhyaḥ, from these. भूतानि Bhûtâni, the gross or great elements. पञ्च Pañcha, five. पञ्चभ्यः Pañchabhyaḥ, from the five. एते Ete, these. स्मृताः Smṛitâḥ, remembered. विशेषाः Viśeṣâḥ, the distinguishables, discernibles, differentiated as pleasant, painful and dull. शान्ताः Śântâḥ, pacific, causing pleasure, tranquil. घोराः Ghorâḥ, terrific, causing pain, disagreeable. च Cha, since. मूढाः Mûḍhâḥ, stupefic, dull. च Cha, and.

XXXVIII. The Tan-mâtras are the indiscernibles. From these five, proceed the five gross Elements which are remembered to be the discernibles; for they are pacific, terrific, and stupefic.

ANNOTATION.

58. Tan-mâtra: *lit.* That-merely or its measure. The Tan-mâtras are subtle forms of Sound, Touch, Form, Taste, and Smell which have

not yet come down to that degree of materialisation in which they cause pleasure, pain, and dulness, and thereby become capable of experience. Such is the force of the word *merely,* according to Vâchaspati's interpretation. They are, however, not properties or qualities but substances. Vijñâna Bhikṣu describes them as "fine substances, the undifferentiated originals of the Gross Elements, which form the substrata of Sound, Touch, Form, Flavour, and Smell, belonging to that class (that is, in that state of their evolution) in which the distinctions of Śânta, etc., do not exist." So we find from the Viṣṇu-Purâṇam and other sources, *e.g.*, that 'in them severally reside their parts (mâtrâ) wherefore the Smṛiti describes them as Tan (their)-mâtra (part). They are neither Śânta, pacific, nor Ghora, terrific, nor, again, Mûḍha, stupefying, but are indistinguishables.'

59. Pacific, etc. :—Every one of the five Gross Elements possesses the threefold characteristic of causing pleasure, pain, and dulness.

Subtile and Gross Bodies described and distinguished.

सूक्ष्मा मातापितृजाः सह प्रभूतैस्त्रिधा विशेषाः स्युः ।
सूक्ष्मास्तेषां नियता मातापितृजा निवर्तन्ते ॥ ३९ ॥

सूक्ष्माः Sûkṣmâḥ subtile Bodies. मातापितृजाः Mâtâ-pitṛi-jâḥ, Bodies produced from mother and father. सह Saha, together. प्रभूतैः Pra-bhûtaiḥ, with the Great Elements. त्रिधा Tri-dhâ, threefold. विशेषाः Viśeṣâḥ, distinguishables, specific objects. स्युः Syuḥ, will be. सूक्ष्माः Sûkṣmâh, subtile Bodies. तेषां Teṣâṃ, among them. नियताः Niyatâḥ constant, continuant. मातापितृजाः Mâtâ-pitṛi-jâḥ, Bodies produced from mother and father. निवर्तन्ते Nivartante, cease, perish.

XXXIX. The Subtile Bodies, Bodies produced from father and mother, together with the Great Elements, will be the Viśeṣas. Amongst them, the Subtile Bodies are continuant ; Bodies produced from father and mother cease (to entangle after death.)

ANNOTATION.

60. Wilson's learned disquisition on the meaning of the present Kârikâ is misguided and misleading. The Sâṃkhya describes or displays the gradual materialisation of the Pradhâna from the highest degree of subtelity to the lowest form of grossness. In the series of evolutes, the Tan-mâtras and the Gross Elements may be said, loosely speaking, to occupy the same plane, that is, the plane of materiality in the current sense of the term, and to stand to each other as do atoms to earth, air,

etc. But though they are on the same plane, there is a marked difference between them; for the Tan-mâtras are indiscernible, while the Elements are discernible. A Viśeṣa is what contains a Viśeṣaṇa or qualification, something extra by means of which it is distinguished from others. In the present case the Viśeṣaṇa is the property of causing pleasure, pain and dulness. This is absent from the Tan-mâtras and is present in the Elements. It is clear, therefore, that the transition from the Tan-mâtras to the next succeeding form of evolution is marked by the development of the property of causing pleasure, pain and dulness. Similarly, the Subtile Body which is a combination of the Tan-mâtras and the Tattvas upward, and Indriyas which are pacific, terrific, and stupefic, contains the aroma of past experiences. So is it as well as the Elements and the Bodies formed of them classed among the Viśeṣas, as distinguished from the Tan-mâtras which are A-Viśeṣas.

How the Subtile Body migrates.

पूर्वोत्पन्नमसक्तं नियतं महदादिसूक्ष्मपर्यन्तम् ।
संसरति निरुपभोगं भावैरधिवासितं लिङ्गम् ॥ ४० ॥

पूर्वोत्पन्नं Pûrva-utpannaṃ, primæval, produced at the beginning of creation by the Pradhâna, one for each Puruṣa. असक्तं A-saktaṃ, unconnected, unconfined to any particular gross Body, and therefore unobstructed in its passage even through a mountain. नियतं Niyataṃ, continuant, constant, as it lasts from the beginning of creation to the time of the Great Dissolution. महदादिसूक्ष्मपर्यन्तम् Mahat-âdi-sûkṣma-paryantam, being the combination of the Tattvas beginning with Mahat and ending with the Subtile, *i.e.*, the Tan-mâtras. संसरति Saṃsarati, moves from Body to Body, transmigrates. निरुपभोगं Nir-upabhogaṃ, free from, or without, experience. भावैः Bhâvaiḥ, dispositions, conditions, such as virtue, vice, etc. अधिवासितं Adhivâsitaṃ, perfumed, affected, tinged. लिङ्गम् Liṅgam, mergent, that which suffers resolution, being a product, a combination of things.

XL. The Liṅga or mergent Body, the one primordially produced, unconfined, continuant, composed of the Tattvas beginning with Mahat and ending with the Tan-mâtras, transmigrates, free from Experience, tinged with the Bhâvas.

ANNOTATION.

61. Tinged with the Bhâvas: The Bhâvas reside in Buddhi which accompanies or is associated with the Subtile Body, and through such association, the Subtile Body is affected by the Bhâvas in the same manner, for instance, as a piece of cloth is perfumed with the sweet smell of a

Champaka flower from contact with it. And it is this affection by the Bhâvas which is the cause of the transmigration of the Subtile Body.

Necessity for Gross Creation shown.

चित्रं यथाश्रयमृते स्थाणवादिभ्यो विना यथाच्छाया ।
तद्वद्विना विशेषैर्न तिष्ठति निराश्रयं लिङ्गम् ॥ ४२ ॥

चित्रं Chitram, a painting or picture. यथा Yathâ, as. आश्रयम् Âśrayam, ground, support. ऋते Ṛite, without. स्थाण्वादिभ्य: Sthâṇu-âdi-bhyaḥ, a stake, etc. विना Vinâ without. यथा Yathâ, as. छाया Chhâyâ, shadow. तद्वत् Tat-vat, similarly to that. विना Vinâ, without. विशेषै: Viśeṣaiḥ, Viśeṣas, Subtile Bodies (Vâchaspati), the Tan-mâtras (Goudapâda), Âtivâhika or Vehicular Bodies (Vijñâna Bhikṣu). न Na, not. तिष्ठति Tiṣṭhati, stands, subsists. निराश्रयं Nir-âśrayam, supportless. लिङ्गम् Lingam, that which makes known, *viz.*, Buddhi, Ahamkâra, Manas and the other Indriyas (Vâchaspati, Gauḍapâda), the Subtile Body called Linga. (Vijñâna).

XLI. As a painting stands not without a support, nor is there a shadow without a stake or the like, so neither does the Linga subsist supportless, without the Viśeṣas.

ANNOTATION.

62. Viśeṣas : The difference of the interpretation of this word points to a difference of doctrine. Thus, according to Gauḍapâda and Vâchaspati, there are only two kinds of Body, as described above. But, according to Vijñâna Bhikṣu, there is also a third kind of Body, the Adhiṣṭhâna Śarîra, which is formed of a finer form of the gross elements and which serves as the receptacle of the Linga Śarîra.

The activity of the Subtile Body further explained.

पुरुषार्थहेतुकमिदं निमित्तनैमित्तिकप्रसंगेन ।
प्रकृतेर्विभुत्वयोगान्नटवद्व्यवतिष्ठते लिङ्गम् ॥ ४२ ॥

पुरुषार्थहेतुकम् Puruṣa-artha-hetu-kam, which has the object of Puruṣa as motive. इदं Idam, this. निमित्तनैमित्तिकप्रसंगेन Nimitta-naimittika-parasangena, by association with instrumental causes such as virtue, vice, etc., and with their consequences such as the body of a god or a man or a beast. प्रकृते: Prakṛiteḥ, of Prakṛiti. विभुत्वयोगात् Vibhu-tva-yogât, from conjunction or the universal supremacy of Prakṛiti. नटवत् Naṭa-vat, like a dramatic actor. व्यवतिष्ठते Vyavatiṣṭhate, appears in different roles. लिङ्गम् Lingam, the subtile body.

XLII. Impelled by the purpose of Puruṣa, this Subtile Body appears in different roles, like a dramatic performer, by means of association with instrumental causes and their consequences, through the universal supremacy of Prakṛiti.

ANNOTATION.

63. Like a dramatic performer: Just as, on the stage, one and the same person plays the parts of Paraśurâma, Ajâtaśatru and Vatsarâja, so the same Subtile Body may appear in the body of a god or an elephant or a man. The final and material causes of this transmigration of the Subtile Body in general are respectively the purpose of Puruṣa and Prakṛiti, and the formal and efficient causes which determine particular migrations, are respectively the consequences of the Nimittas and the Nimittas, namely, virtue, vice, and the like.

Bhâvas divided and described.

सांसिद्धिकाश्च भावाः प्राकृतिका वैकृतिकाश्च धर्माद्याः ।
दृष्टाः करणाश्रयिणः कार्याश्रयिणश्च कललाद्याः ॥४३॥

सांसिद्धिका : Sâṃsiddhikâḥ, produced from means already in existence, *viz.*, previous Karma; innate, instinctive. च Cha, and. भावाः Bhâvâḥ, dispositions, conditions, circumstances. प्राकृतिकाः Prâkṛitikâḥ, essential, natural, springing from Prâkṛiti direct. वैकृतिकाः Vaikṛitikâḥ, acquired, due or relating to vikṛiti or transformations. च Cha, and. धर्माद्याः Dharma-âdyâḥ, virtue and the rest. दृष्टाः Driṣṭâḥ, seen. करणाश्रयिणः Karaṇa-âśrâyiṇaḥ, residing in the Karaṇa, *i.e*, Buddhi. कार्याश्रयिणः Kârya-âsrayiṇaḥ, residing in the effect, *i.e*, body. च Cha, and. कललाद्याः Kalala-âdyâḥ, the uterine germ and the rest.

XLIII. The Bhâvas or dispositions are instinctive, essential, and also acquired. Dharma and the rest are considered as residing in Buddhi, and the uterine germ and the rest as residing in the Body.

ANNOTATION.

64. *Sâṃsiddhika*: as, at the beginning of creation, when the Lord Kapila was to appear, the four Bhâvas, *viz.*, virtue, knowledge, dispassion, and power, were produced along with him. They are then the effects of causes appertaining to a former creation.

Prâkṛitika: These are equally innate or instinctive, but are the effects of causes appertaining to the present creation. Thus, from the very same causes, *i.e.*, highly purified form of Prakṛitic matter, from which the perpetually youthful Bodies of the four sons of Brahmâ, namely, Śanaka, Sanandana, Sanâtana, and Sanatkumâra, were produced, were also at the same time produced the Bhâvas of virtue and the rest in them.

Vaikṛitika: These are those acquired from a Vikṛiti or evolute, namely, a teacher whose Body is an evolute; thus the effect of tuition is knowledge, knowledge leads to dispassion, dispassion to virtue, and virtue to power. This is how ordinary human beings acquire the Bhâvas.

The Bhâvas, virtue, knowledge, dispassion, and power, grow when Sattva is dominant. Hence they are characterised as Sâttvic. Those that grow during the predominance of Tamas, are vice, ignorance, passion, and weakness. These are characterised as Tâmasic.

These eight Bhâvas are the Nimittas or efficient causes of particular migrations of the Liṅga Śarira. They operate through bringing about connection with their effects, the Naimittikas, from the first commingled blood and semen in the uterus up to the fully developed Body.

Effects of the Bhâvas described.

धर्मेण गमनमूर्द्ध्वं गमनमधस्ताद्भवत्यधर्मेण ।
ज्ञानेन चापवर्गो विपर्ययादिष्यते बन्धः ॥ ४४ ॥

धर्मेण Dharmeṇa, by means of virtue. गमनम् Gamanam, going. ऊर्द्ध्वं Urdhvaṃ, upward. गमनम् Gamanam, going. अधस्तात् Adhastât, downward. भवति Bhavati, is. अधर्मेण A-dharmeṇa, by means of vice. ज्ञानेन Jñânena, by means of knowledge. च Cha, and. अपवर्गः Apavargaḥ, release. विपर्ययात् Viparyayât, from the reverse, *i.e.*, of knowledge, that is, ignorance. इष्यते Iṣyate, considered. बन्धः Bandhaḥ, bondage.

XLIV. By virtue, is going upward; going downward is by vice; and by knowledge, is Release; from the reverse, Bondage is considered (to be.)

ANNOTATION.

65. Upwards: that is, to the worlds of Brahmâ, Prajâpati, Soma, Indra, the Gandharvas, the Yakṣas, the Râkṣasas, and the Piśâchas.

Downward: that is, into the Bodies of beasts, birds, reptiles, trees, etc.

Knowledge: that is, knowledge of the discrimination between Puruṣa and Prakṛiti.

Release: when the Subtile Body ceases and Puruṣa becomes Paramaâtmâ.

Bondage: it is either Prâkṛitika, or Vaikṛitika, or Dâkṣiṇaka. The first is of those who, mistaking either of the eight Prakṛitis, *viz.*, the Pradhâna, Mahat, Ahaṃkâra, and the five Tan-mâtras, to be Puruṣa, contemplate upon that, and not upon Puruṣa. After death, they are absorbed in the Prakṛitis, and are called Prakṛiti-layas. The second is of those who contemplate upon the transformations, *viz.*, the elements, the Indriyas, individual Ahaṃkâra and individual Buddhi, mistaking them for Puruṣa, and after death reach unto the archetypes of those transformations. The third is of those who, not knowing the Tattva, *i.e.*, Puruṣa, seek mundane and heavenly happiness through performance of acts of charity and public utility.

Above continued.

वैराग्यात् प्रकृतिलयः संसारो भवति राजसाद्रागात् ।
ऐश्वर्यादविघातो विपर्ययात्तद्विपर्यासः ॥ ४५ ॥

वैराग्यात् Vairâgyât, from dispassion, that is, from dispassion divorced from knowledge of the Tattvas. प्रकृतिलयः Prakṛiti-layaḥ, absorption into the eight Prakṛitis, which state of absorption lasts for full one hundred thousand Manvantaras. संसारः Samsâraḥ, transmigration, revolution of births and deaths. भवति Bhavati, is. राजसात् Râjasât, produced from, or appertaining to, Rajas. रागात् Râgât, from passion. ऐश्वर्यात् Aiśvaryât, from power. अविघातः A-vighâtaḥ, non-impediment *i.e.*, of desire. विपर्ययात् Viparyayât, from the reverse, *i.e.*, from weakness. तद्विपर्यासः Tat-viparyâsaḥ, the contrary thereof, *i e.* impediment.

XLV. From dispassion is absorption into the Prakṛitis, transmigration is from the passion of Rajas, from power is unimpediment, from the reverse is the contrary.

ANNOTATION.

66. In these two Kârikâs, the eight efficient causes and their eight effects have been declared. They are:

	CAUSE.	EFFECT.
Sattvic	1. Virtue.	2. Elevation to the higher worlds.
	3. Knowledge.	4. Release.
	5. Dispassion.	6. Dissolution into the Prakṛitis.
	7. Power.	8. Unimpediment to fulfilment of desire.
Tamasic	9. Vice.	10. Degradation to the lower worlds.
	11. Ignorance.	12. Bondage.
	13. Passion.	14. Migration.
	15. Weakness.	16. Impediment to fulfilment of desire.

The creations of Buddhi classified and explained.

एषो प्रत्ययसर्गो विपर्ययाशक्तितुष्टिसिद्ध्याख्यः ।
गुणवैषम्यविमर्दात्तस्य च भेदास्तु पञ्चाशत् ॥ ४६ ॥

एषः Eṣaḥ, this. प्रत्ययसर्गः Pratyaya-sargaḥ, the creation of that by which intuition of things is made, that is, Buddhi. विपर्ययाशक्तितुष्टिसिद्ध्याख्यः viparyâya-aśakti-tuṣṭi-siddhi-âkhyaḥ, called ignorance, incapacity, complacency, and perfection.

गुणवैषम्यविमर्दात् Guṇa-vaiṣamya-vimardât, from the conflict of the Guṇas in unequal degrees of strength, from the combination of the Guṇas in different proportions, and consequent predominance of one over others. तस्य Tasya, its, of the creation of Buddhi. च Cha and. भेदाः Bhedâḥ, sorts, divisions. तु Tu, again. पञ्चाशत् Pañchâśat, fifty.

XLVI. This is the creation of Buddhi, termed ignorance, incapacity, complacency, and perfection. And from the conflict of the Guṇas in unequal degree of strength, its sorts, again, are fifty.

ANNOTATION.

67. This : that is, the sixteenfold cause and effect mentioned in the preceding Kârikâ. They are all modifications or products of Buddhi. Their minor divisions are legions. To attempt some classification, they are primarily of four sorts, and secondarily of fifty sorts.

The creations of Buddhi subdivided.

पञ्च विपर्ययभेदा भवन्त्यशक्तिश्च करणवैकल्यात् ।
अष्टाविंशतिभेदा तुष्टिर्नवधाऽष्टधा सिद्धिः ॥ ४७ ॥

पञ्च Pañcha, five, *viz.*, A-vidyâ, Asmitâ, Râga, Dveṣa, and Abhiniveṣa. विपर्ययभेदाः Viparyaya-bhedâḥ, divisions of mistake or ignorance. भवन्ति Bhavanti, are. अशक्तिः A-śaktiḥ, incapacity. च Cha, and. करणवैकल्यात् Karaṇa-vaikalyât, according to the impairment of the Instruments or Indriyas. अष्टाविंशतिभेदा Aṣṭâvimśati-bhedâ, having twenty-eight divisions. तुष्टिः Tuṣṭiḥ, complacency. नवधा Nava-dhâ, ninefold. अष्टधा Aṣṭa-dhâ, eightfold. सिद्धिः Siddhiḥ, perfection.

XLVII. Five are the divisions of ignorance ; and according to the impairment of the instruments, incapacity has twenty-eight varieties ; while complacency is ninefold ; perfection, eightfold.

Divisions of Error subdivided.

भेदस्तमसोऽष्टविधो मोहस्य च दशविधो महामोहः ।
तामिस्रोऽष्टादशधा तथा भवत्यन्धतामिस्रः ॥ ४८ ॥

भेदाः Bhedâḥ, distinctions, divisions. तमसः Tamasaḥ, of Tamas, which is a technical term for A-Vidyâ or false knowledge. अष्टविधः Aṣṭa-vidhaḥ, eightfold. मोहस्य Mohasya, of Moha, which is technical for Asmitâ or Am-ness or egotism. च Cha and. दशविधः Daśa-vidhaḥ, tenfold. महामोहः Mahâ-mohaḥ, Mahâmoha, which is technical for Râga or passion. तामिस्रः Tâmisraḥ, Tâmisra, which is technical for Dveṣa or aversion. अष्टादशधा Aṣṭâdaśa-dhâ, eighteenfold. तथा Tathâ, so. भवति Bhavâti, is. अन्धतामिस्रः Andha-tâmisraḥ. Andhatâmisra, which is technical for Abhiniveśa or blind attachment to life.

XLVIII. The distinctions of A-Vidyâ are eightfold, as also of Asmitâ ; tenfold is Râga ; Dveṣa is eighteenfold ; so also is Abhiniveśa.

Incapacity subdivided.

एकादशेन्द्रियवधाः सह बुद्धिवधैरशक्तिरुद्दिष्टा ।
सप्तदश वधा बुद्धेर्विपर्ययात्तुष्टिसिद्धीनाम् ॥ ४९ ॥

एकादशेन्द्रियवधाः Ekâdaśa-indriya-badhâḥ, injuries of the eleven Indriyas. सह Saha, together. बुद्धिवधैः Buddhi-badhaiḥ, with injuries of Buddhi. अशक्तिः A-śaktiḥ incapacity. उद्दिष्टा Uddiṣṭâ, pronounced. सप्तदशवधाः Saptadaśa-badhâḥ, seventeen injuries. बुद्धेः Buddheḥ, of Buddhi. विपर्ययात् Viparyayât, from inversion. तुष्टिसिद्धीनाम् Tuṣti-siddhînâm, of complacencies and perfections.

XLIX. Injuries of the eleven Indriyas, together with injuries of Buddhi, are pronounced to be Incapacity. The injuries of Buddhi are seventeen, through inversion of complacencies and perfections.

Complacency subdivided.

आध्यात्मिकाश्चतस्रः प्रकृत्युपादानकालभाग्याख्याः ।
बाह्या विषयोपरमात् पञ्च नव तुष्टयोऽभिमताः ॥ ५० ॥

आध्यात्मिका: Âdhyâtmikâḥ, self (soul)-regarding, it is that form of complacency in which there is belief in the existence of a Self, as distinct from Prakṛiti, but in which the Self is identified with the Not-Self. चतस्रः Chatasra, four. प्रकृत्युपादानकालभाग्याख्याः Prakṛiti-upâdâna-kâla-bhâgya-âkhyâḥ, called after Prakṛiti or Root, Upâdâna or Material, Kâla or Time, and Bhâgya or Luck. बाह्याः Bâhyâḥ, external, Not-Self-regarding. विषयोपरमात् Viṣaya-uparamât, through abstinence from objects. पञ्च Pañcha, five. नवधा Nava-dhâ, ninefold. तुष्टयः Tuṣṭayaḥ, complacencies. अभिहिताः Abhihitâḥ, propounded.

L. The nine Complacencies are propounded : the four Self-regarding ones called after Prakṛiti, Material, Time, and Luck ; the external five, through abstinence from objects.

Perfection subdivided.

ऊहः शब्दोऽध्ययनं दुःखविघातास्त्रयः सुहृत्प्राप्तिः ।
दानं च सिद्धयोऽष्टौ सिद्धेः पूर्वोऽङ्कुशस्त्रिविधः ॥ ५१ ॥

ऊहः Uhaḥ, reasoning, argumentation. शब्दः Śabdaḥ, word, verbal instruction. अध्ययनं Adhyayanam, study. दुःखविघाताः Duḥkha-vighâtâḥ, preventions of pain. त्रयः Trayaḥ, three. सुहृत्प्राप्तिः Suhṛit-prâptiḥ, acquisition of friend, intercourse with friend. दानं Dânam, charity, purity. च Cha, and. सिद्धयः Siddhayaḥ, perfections. अष्टौ Aṣṭau, eight. सिद्धेः Siddheḥ, of perfection. पूर्वः Pûrvaḥ, preceding, first. अङ्कुशः Aṅkuśaḥ, goad, curb, restrainer. त्रिविधः Tri-Vidhaḥ, threefold.

LI. Argumentation, Word, Study, the three Preventions of Pain, Acquisition of friends, Charity or Purity are the eight Perfections. Those mentioned before Perfection are the threefold goad to (Ignorance and suffering).

ANNOTATION.

68. Those mentioned before Perfection are Ignorance, Incapacity, and Complacency.

Aṅkuśa :—This word may also be rendered by curb, meaning that Ignorance and the rest curb, *i.e.*, impede or obstruct the means to Perfection.

69. Vijñâna Bhikṣu has interpreted this Kârikâ in a different manner and has criticised unfavourably the exposition of Gauḍapâda and Vâchaspati. See our Sâṃkhya-Pravachana-Sûtram, Sacred Books of the Hindus, Vol. XI, page 321.

70. The above details of the creations of Buddhi have been fully explained in the commentaries on the Tattva-Samâsaḥ and the Sâṃkhya Pravachana-Sûtraṃ. The reader is accordingly referred to Vol. XI of the Sacred Books of the Hindus.

71. Now, if it be questioned that when any one of the two, *viz.*, creations of Buddhi and creations of the Tan-mâtras, is enough for the accomplishment of the purpose of Puruṣa, what need is there for a twofold creation ? so it is declared in the succeeding Kârikâ.

Twofold creation, of Buddhi and of Tanmâtra, upheld.

न विना भावैर्लिङ्गं न विना लिङ्गेन भावनिर्वृत्तिः ।
लिङ्गाख्यो भावाख्यस्तस्माद्द्विविधः प्रवर्तते सर्गः ॥ ५२ ॥

न Na, not. विना Vinâ, without. भावैः Bhâvaiḥ, dispositions, the creations of Buddhi mentioned above. लिङ्गं Liṅgaṃ, the creation of the Tan-mâtras. न

Na, not. विना Vinâ, without. लिङ्गेन Lingena, the creation of the Tan-mâtras. भावनिर्वृत्तिः Bhâva-nirvrittiḥ, cessation or pause of the dispositions. लिङ्गाख्यः Linga-âkhyaḥ, termed Linga. भावाख्यः Bhâva-âkhyaḥ, termed Bhâva. तस्मात् Tasmât, hence. द्विविधः Dvi-vidhaḥ, twofold. प्रवर्तते Pravartate, proceeds. सर्गः Sargaḥ, creation.

LII. Without the Bhâvas, there would be no Linga, without the Linga, there would be no surcease of the Bhâvas; wherefrom a twofold creation proceeds; the one called after the Linga, the other called after the Bhâvas.

ANNOTATION.

72. Vâchaspati explains the necessity for a twofold creation and their interdependence thus: Experience which is the object of Purusa, cannot be possible in the absence of the objects of experience, such as sound and the rest, as well as of the twofold Body which is the Âyatana or house of experience: wherefore the creations of the Tan-mâtras are necessary. In the same manner, the very same Experience is not possible without the Indriyas and the Antaḥ-karaṇa which are the instruments of Experience; these, again, cannot be possible without the Bhâvas, virtue and the rest. Neither is the manifestation of Discrimination, which is the cause of Release, possible in the absence of the twofold creation. Hence the twofold creation is established.

The succession of the two kinds of creation as mutually cause and effect is no fault, as it is from eternity, like that of the seed and the sprout. Even in the beginning of a Kalpa the production of the Bhâvas and the Linga under the influence of the Samskâra or impression of the Bhâvas and the Linga produced in a previous Kalpa, is not unproved.

Gross Creation subdivided.

अष्टविकल्पो दैवस्तैर्यग्योनश्च पञ्चधा भवति ।
मानुष्यश्चैकविधः समासतोऽयं भौतिकः सर्गः ॥ ५३ ॥

अष्टविकल्पः Asta-vikalpaḥ, having eight specific kinds, *viz.*, Brâhma, Prâjâpatya, etc. दैवः Daivaḥ, divine, celestial, supernatural, super-human. तैर्यग्योनः Tairyak-yonaḥ, the grovelling-born. च Cha, and. पञ्चधा Pañcha-dhâ, fivefold. भवति Bhavati, is. मानुष्यः Mânusyaḥ, human. च Cha, and, while. एकविधः Eka-vidhaḥ, uniform, of one kind. समासतः Samâsa-taḥ, briefly. अयं Ayam, this. भौतिकः Bhautikaḥ, of the Bhûtas or beings. सर्गः Sargaḥ, creation.

LIII. The superhuman is of eight kinds; and the grovelling species is of five kinds; and the human is of a single kind ; this, briefly, is the Bhautika Sarga or Creation of Beings.

Higher, Lower, and Intermediate Worlds characterised.

ऊर्द्ध्वं सत्त्वविशालस्तमोविशालश्च मूलतः सर्गः ।
मध्ये रजोविशालो ब्रह्मादिस्तम्बपर्यन्तः ॥ ५४ ॥

ऊर्द्ध्वं Urddhvam, above, in the higher worlds of Brahma and the rest. सत्त्वविशालः Sattva-viśâlaḥ, abundant in Sattva, in which Sattva is dominant and Rajas and Tamas are dormant. तमोविशालः Tamaḥ-viśâlaḥ, abundant in Tamas, in which Tamas is dominant and Sattva and Rajas are dormant. च Cha, and. मूलतः Mûla-taḥ, at the bottom, below.

सर्गः Sargaḥ, creation. मध्ये Madhye, in the middle, in the world of man. रजोविशालः Rajaḥ-viśâlaḥ, abundant in Rajas, in which Rajas is dominant and Sattva and Tamas are dormant. ब्रह्मादिस्तम्बपर्यन्तः Brahma-âdi-stamba-paryantaḥ, beginning with Brahmâ and ending with a stock.

LIV. Above, the creation is abundant in Sattva; below, it is abundant in Tamas ; in the middle, it is abundant in Rajas ; such is the creation from Brahmâ down to a stock.

Universality of pain demonstrated.

तत्र जरामरणकृतं दुःखं प्राप्नोति चेतनः पुरुषः ।
लिङ्गस्याविनिवृत्तेस्तस्माद्दुःखं स्वभावेन ॥ ५५ ॥

तत्र Tatra, therein, in the three worlds, in the bodies of the superhuman, human and grovelling species. जरामरणकृतं Jarâ-maraṇa-kṛitam, caused by decay and death. दुःखं Duḥkham, pain. प्राप्नोति Prâpnoti, experiences. चेतनः Chetanaḥ, intelligent. The force of this word is to exclude experience of pain from Prakṛiti and her products which are all non-intelligent. पुरुषः Puruṣaḥ, that which lies (*Sete*) in the *Puri* or the Liṅga Śarîra or Subtile Body, Puruṣa. लिङ्गस्य Liṅga-sya, of the Liṅga Śarîra. अविनिवृत्तेः A-vinivṛitteḥ, owing to the non-cessation, or till the cessation of the Liṅga Śarîra which is continuant (see Kârikâ XL), and does not cease till the development of discriminative knowledge. तस्मात् Tasmât, therefore. दुःखं Duḥkham, pain. स्वभावेन Sva-bhâvena, by nature.

LV. Therein does intelligent Puruṣa experience pain caused by decay and death, on acount of the non-cessation of, or till the cessation of, the Subtile Body : wherefore pain is the natural order of things.

Object of Prakṛiti's creation explained.

इत्येषः प्रकृतिकृतो महदादिविशेषभूतपर्यन्तः ।
प्रतिपुरुषविमोक्षार्थं स्वार्थ इव परार्थ आरम्भः ॥ ५६ ॥

इति Iti, thus then. एषः Eṣaḥ, this. प्रकृतिकृतः Prakṛiti-kṛitaḥ, originated by Prakṛiti. महदादिविशेषभूतपर्यन्तः Mahat-âdi-viśeṣa-bhûta-paryantaḥ, beginning with Mahat and ending with the particular, *i.e.*, gross elemental creations. प्रतिपुरुषविमोक्षार्थं Pratipuruṣa-arthaṃ, for the release of each individual Puruṣa. स्वार्थे Svà-arthe, in her own interest. इव Iva, as. परार्थे Para-arthe, in the interest of another, *i.e.*, of Puruṣa. आरम्भः Ârambhaḥ, creation.

LVI. Thus then is this creation beginning with Mahat and ending with specific entities, originated by Prakṛiti in the interest of another as in her own interest, for the release of each individual Puruṣa.

ANNOTATION.

73. Originated by Prakṛiti: Creation by Prakṛiti is not guided, directed, and controlled by Îśvara or Âdi Puruṣa, for this is impossible, inasmuch as no activity can belong to him. Neither can Brahman be the material of creation, for, being the power or energy of Consciousness, it can undergo no transformation or modification.

For the release of each individual Puruṣa: This explains why, on the release of one Puruṣa, the release of others does not result, and how the activity of Prakṛiti whose nature is to energise, can cease in regard to a particular Puruṣa, and how creation does not ever continue, making release of any one impossible. Vâchaspati explains the passage thus: As a man who desires food, being engaged in the cooking of food, rests after the food has been cooked, so does Prakṛiti, who is engaged in activity with a view to release every individual Puruṣa, cease from energising again in regard to that Puruṣa whom she releases.

Spontaniety of Prakṛiti explained and illustrated.

वत्सविवृद्धिनिमित्तं क्षीरस्य यथा प्रवृत्तिरज्ञस्य ।
पुरुषविमोक्षनिमित्तं तथा प्रवृत्तिः प्रधानस्य ॥ ५७ ॥

वत्सविवृद्धिनिमित्तं Vatsa-vivṛiddhi-nimittaṃ, for the sake of, or due to the nourishment of, the calf. क्षीरस्य Kṣîra-sya, of milk. यथा Yathâ, as. प्रवृत्तिः Pravṛittiḥ, activity, *i.e.*, secretion. अज्ञस्य A-jña-sya, of the unintelligent. पुरुषविमोक्षनिमित्तं Puruṣa-vimokṣa-nimittaṃ, due to the release of Puruṣa. तथा Tathâ, so. प्रवृत्तिः Pravṛittiḥ, activity, *i.e.*, creation. प्रधानस्य Pradhâna-sya, of the Pradhâna.

LVII. Just as is the secretion of milk, which is unintelligent, for the sake of nourishment of the calf, so is the creation of the Pradhâna for the sake of the release of Puruṣa.

ANNOTATION.

74. This Kârikâ gives an answer to those who entertain doubts as to how an unintelligent substance such as Prakṛiti is represented here to be, can engage in activity for an altruistic end. It cannot be maintained that the secretion of milk takes place under the superintendence of Îśvara. For all intelligent activity such as, for instance, as is here attributed to Îśvara, proceeds either from selfish motives or from compassion. Now, in the case of Îśvara, who is *exhypothesi* all-full, having all desires fulfilled, wanting in nothing whatever, can possibly have no selfish ends to accomplish. Compassion also is impossible; for compassion implies the desire to alleviate, remove or prevent suffering, but prior to creation there is no existence of the Jîvas, Indriyas, Bodies, and Objects, and consequently no pain, no suffering. Compassion, therefore, cannot be the motive for creation. Further, were creation an act of compassion on the part of Îśvara, one would expect to find in it only happy beings, but such is not the case, but just the opposite. The anomaly cannot be explained by reference to diversity of Karma, as in that case the alleged superintendence of Karma by an omniscient and omnipotent Being falls to the ground. Prakṛiti, on the other hand, being unintelligent, has no selfish motive nor any motive of compassion to impel her to activity. Her activity is directed simply by the end of the other; she exists for his sake. Her action is of the nature of a sympathetic response, of harmonical variation or correspondence, like the secretion of the mother's milk, in response to the requirement of the baby.

Above continued.

औत्सुक्यनिवृत्त्यर्थं यथा क्रियासु प्रवर्तते लोकः ।
पुरुषस्य विमोक्षार्थं प्रवर्तते तद्वदव्यक्तम् ॥ ५८ ॥

औत्सुक्यनिवृत्त्यर्थं Autsukya-nivritti-artham, for the sake of relieving or gratifying desire or curiosity. यथा Yathâ, as. क्रियासु Kriyâsu, in acts. प्रवर्तते Pravartate, engages. लोकः Lokaḥ, man. पुरुषस्य Puruṣa-sya, of Puruṣa. विमोक्षार्थं Vimokṣa-artham, for the sake of release. प्रवर्तते Pravartate, energises. तद्वत् Tat-vat, similarly to this. अव्यक्तम् A-Vyaktam, the Unmanifest, Prakṛiti.

LVIII. Just as people engage in acts to relieve

anxiety or desires, so does the Unmanifest energise for the purpose of the release of Puruṣa.

How Prakṛiti's creation ceases spontaneously.

रङ्गस्य दर्शयित्वा निवर्तते नर्तकी यथा नृत्यात् ।
पुरुषस्य तथात्मानं प्रकाश्य निवर्तते प्रकृतिः ॥ ५९ ॥

रङ्गस्य Raṅga-sya, to the stage, *i.e.*, the spectators. दर्शयित्वा Darśayitvâ, having exhibited. निवर्तते Nivartate, ceases, desists. नर्तकी Nartaki, fair dancer. यथा Yathâ, as. नृत्यात् Nṛityât, from dance. पुरुषस्य Puruṣa-sya, to Puruṣa. तथा Tathâ, similarly. आत्मानं Âtmânaṃ, herself. प्रकाश्य Prakâśya, having exhibited. निवर्तते Nivartate, ceases. प्रकृतिः Prakṛitiḥ, Prakṛiti.

LIX. Just as a fair dancer, having exhibited herself to the spectators, desists from the dance, so does Prakṛiti desist, having exhibited herself to Puruṣa.

Unselfishness of Prakṛiti demonstrated.

नानाविधैरुपायैरुपकारिण्यनुपकारिणः पुंसः ।
गुणवत्यगुणस्य सतस्तस्यार्थमपार्थकं चरति ॥ ६० ॥

नानाविधैः Nânâ-vidhaiḥ, manifold. उपायैः Upâyaiḥ, by means. उपकारिणी Upakâriṇi, generous, beneficent. अनुपकारिणः An-upakâriṇaḥ, non-beneficent, ungrateful. पुंसः Puṃsaḥ, of Puruṣa. गुणवती Guṇa-vatî, possessing the Guṇas, possessing qualities, virtuous. अगुणस्य A-guṇa-sya, devoid of the Guṇas, devoid of qualities, worthless. सतः Sataḥ, as he is. तस्य Tasya, his. अर्थं Artham, object. अपार्थकं Ap-artha-kaṃ, objectless. चरति Charati, pursues.

LX. By manifold means does benevolent Prakṛiti, possessed of the Guṇas, pursue, in a manner in which she has no interest of her own, the object of Puruṣa who makes no return, being devoid as he is of the Guṇas.

How activity of Prakṛiti ceases for ever, in regard to the released Puruṣa.

प्रकृतेः सुकुमारतरं न किञ्चिदस्तीति मे मतिर्भवति ।
या दृष्टास्मीति पुनर्न दर्शनमुपैति पुरुषस्य ॥ ६१ ॥

प्रकृते: Prakṛiteḥ, than Prakṛiti. सुकुमारतरं Sukumâra-taraṃ, more gentle or delicate. न Na, not. किञ्चित् Kiṃ chit, anything. अस्ति Asti, exists. इति Iti, such. मे Me, my. मतिः Matiḥ, opinion. भवति Bhavati, is. या Yâ, who. दृष्टा Dṛiṣṭâ, seen.

अस्मि Asmi, I am. इति Iti, so. पुनः Punaḥ, again. न Na, not. दर्शनम् Darśanam, seeing, gaze, sight. उपैति Upaiti, approaches. पुरुषस्य Puruṣa-sya, of Puruṣa.

LXI. My opinion is that nothing exists which is more delicate than Prakṛiti who, knowing that, "I have seen," comes no more within the sight of Puruṣa.

ANNOTATION.

75. This Kârikâ explains and illustrates how Prakṛiti does not energise, over again, in regard to the released Puruṣa.

Bondage, Transmigration and Release are all of Prakṛiti, and not of Puruṣa.

तस्मान्न बध्यतेऽद्धा न मुच्यते नापि संसरति पुरुषः ।
संसरति बध्यते मुच्यते च नानाश्रया प्रकृतिः ॥ ६२ ॥

तस्मात् Tasmât, therefore. न Na, not. बध्यते Badhyate, is bound. अद्धा Addhâ, any, whatever. न Na, not. मुच्यते Muchyate, is released. न Na, not. अपि Api, also. संसरति Saṃsarati, transmigrates. पुरुषः Puruṣaḥ, Puruṣa. संसरति Saṃsarati, transmigrates. बध्यते Badhyate, is bound. मुच्यते Muchyate, is released. च Cha, and. नानाश्रया Nânâ-âśrayâ, the support of manifold creations or beings. प्रकृतिः Prakṛitiḥ, Prakṛiti.

LXII. Wherefore, verily, no Puruṣa is ever bound, nor is released, nor transmigrates. Prakṛiti, being the support of manifold creations, is bound, is released, and transmigrates.

How Prakṛiti binds and releases herself.

रूपैः सप्तभिरेव तु बध्नात्यात्मानमात्मना प्रकृतिः ।
सैव च पुरुषार्थं प्रति विमोचयत्येकरूपेण ॥ ६३ ॥

रूपैः Rûpaiḥ, by forms, modes, conditions, dispositions. सप्तभिः Saptabhiḥ, seven, *viz.* virtue, vice, dispassion, passion, power, weakness, and ignorance. एव Eva, verily. बध्नाति Badhnâti, binds. आत्मानम् Âtmânam, herself, आत्मना Âtmanâ, by herself. प्रकृतिः Prakṛitiḥ, Prakṛiti. सा Sâ, she. एव Eva, it is. च Cha, and. पुरुषार्थं Puruṣa-arthaṃ, object of Puruṣa. प्रति Prati, in regard to. विमोचयति vimochayati, releases. एकरूपेण Eka-rûpeṇa, by one form, *i. e.*, of Knowledge.

LXIII. By seven forms does Prakṛiti bind herself by herself; and it is she who, by one form, releases herself for the sake of Puruṣa.

How discriminative knowledge is fully developed.

एवं तत्त्वाभ्यासान्नास्ति न मे नाहमित्यपरिशेषम् ।
अविपर्ययाद्विशुद्धं केवलमुत्पद्यते ज्ञानम् ॥ ६४ ॥

एवं Evaṃ, so, in the manner, taught above. तत्त्वाभ्यासात् Tattva-abhyâsât, through cultivation of the knowledge of the Tattvas or twenty-five Principles. न Na, not. अस्ति Asti, is. न Na, not. मे Me, mine. न Na, not. अहम् Aham, I. इति Iti, thus. अपरिशेषम् Apariśeṣam, beyond which there remains nothing to know, final. अविपर्ययात् A-viparyayât, from the absence of error and doubt. विशुद्धं Viśuddham, purified, free. केवलम् Kevalam, single, unsullied. उत्पद्यते Utpadyate, is produced. ज्ञानम् Jñânam, knowledge.

LXIV. So, through cultivation of the knowledge of the Tattvas, is produced the final, pure, because free from error and doubt, and one single knowledge that neither does agency belong to me, nor is attachment mine, nor am I identical with the Body, etc.

Relation of Prakṛiti and Puruṣa after Release.

तेन निवृत्तप्रसवामर्थवशात् सप्तरूपविनिवृत्ताम् ।
प्रकृतिं पश्यति पुरुषः प्रेक्षकवदवस्थितः स्वस्थः ॥ ६५ ॥

तेन Tena, thereby, by means of knowledge of the Tattvas, as described in the preceding Kârikâ. निवृत्तप्रसवाम् Nivṛitta-prasavâm, whose prolificness has come to cease through creation of all that was to be created for the sake of Puruṣa. अर्थवशात् Artha-vaśât, through the influence of the object, *viz.*, knowledge of the Tattvas. सप्तरूपविनिवृत्ताम् Sapta-rûpa-vinivṛittâm, desisting from the seven forms, virtue and the rest, by which she binds herself and which are no longer required for the sake of Puruṣa, both of whose objects, experience and release, are accomplished. प्रकृतिं Prakṛitim, Prakṛiti. पश्यति Paśyati, looks at. पुरुषः Puruṣaḥ, Puruṣa. प्रेक्षकवत् Prekṣaka-vat, like a spectator in a theatre. अवस्थितः Avasthitaḥ, seated, standing by. स्वस्थः Sva-sthaḥ, self-reposed, undisturbed, freed from the reflection of Buddhi rendered impure by means of the modifications of Rajas and Tamas.

LXV. Thereby having her prolific energy stopped, and desisting from the seven forms under the influence of knowledge, Prakṛiti is looked at by Puruṣa just like a spectator, standing by, self-reposed.

Conjunction of Prakṛiti and Puruṣa is not, as such, the cause of creation.

दृष्टा मयेत्युपेक्षक एको दृष्टाहमित्युपरमत्यन्या ।
सति संयोगेऽपि तयोः प्रयोजनं नास्ति सर्गस्य ॥ ६६ ॥

दृष्टा Driṣṭâ, seen. मया Mayâ, by me. इति Iti, so. उपेक्षकः Upekṣakaḥ, regardless, indifferent, unaffected. एकः Ekaḥ, the one, Puruṣa. दृष्टा Driṣṭâ, seen. अहम् Aham, I. इति Iti, so. उपरमति Uparamati, desists. अन्या Anyâ, the other, Prakṛiti. सति Sati, existing, continuing. संयोगे Saṃyoge, conjunction, existence side by side. अपि Api, even. तयोः Tayoḥ of the two. प्रयोजनं Prayojanaṃ, purpose, motive. न Na, not. अस्ति, Exists. सर्गस्य Sarga-sya, of creation.

LXVI. "She has been seen by me,"—so the one stands indifferent; "I have been seen,"—so the other desists. Though their conjunction still remains, there does not exist any motive for creation.

Jîvàn-Mukti explained.

सम्यग्ज्ञानाधिगमाद्धर्मादीनामकारणप्राप्तौ ।
तिष्ठति संस्कारवशाच्चक्रभ्रमवद्धृतशरीरः ॥ ६७ ॥

सम्यक् Samyak, perfect. ज्ञानाधिगमात् Jñâna-adhigamât, from attainment of knowledge. धर्मादीनाम् Dharma-âdînâm, of virtue and the rest. अकारणप्राप्तौ A-kâraṇa-prâptau, on reaching or being reduced to the state in which they lose their power of causing effects. तिष्ठति Tiṣṭhati, remains. संस्कारवशात् Saṃskâra-vaśât, from the influence of Saṃskâra or impression or the effect of the impulse previously given to it. चक्रभ्रमवत् Chakra-bhrama-vat, like the whirling of the potter's wheel. धृतशरीरः Dhṛita-śarîraḥ, invested with a Body.

LXVII. Through attainment of perfect knowledge, virtue and the rest coming to be deprived of their power as causes, Puruṣa yet continues invested with body under the influence of previous Dharma and A-Dharma, as the potter's wheel continues whirling (from momentum).

ANNOTATION.

76. This Kârikâ explains the fact of Jîvan-Mukti or release in life, as in the case of Kapila, Vâmadeva, and others. Jîvan-Mukti consists in the release of an incarnate Puruṣa from the entanglement of Prakṛiti prior to his separation from the Body. These two things, *viz.*, release from bondage and continuance of the Body, are compatible with each other, as they are dependent upon independent causes. For, universally, release

takes place on the manifestation of discriminative knowledge between Prakṛiti and Puruṣa, in other words, it does not imply the acquisition of a new state or condition, but consists merely in the removal of a veil or a shadow, as it were ; whereas the Body is the positive result of positive causes and depends for its existence or non-existence upon those very causes. These causes are Dharma and A-Dharma, or merit and demerit, collectively termed Karma. Now, 'Karma is distinguished as Prârabdha or operative, Sañchita or stored or potential, and Agamika, or to come, or future. On the attainment of discriminative knowledge, Sañchita Karma or Karma in seed-form is burnt up and rendered infructuous, and Âgamika Karma also is necessarily precluded. Only the Prârabdha then remains. It is Karma acquired by acts performed in a previous life and which has become operative in the present life, that is to say, it is the cause of conjunction with the present Body and of all the experiences of the present incarnate existence. It is not affected by discriminative knowledge, and it goes on sustaining the Body till it is exhausted or works itself out, in its natural course, when the Body which was supported by it, automatically drops down. It is hence, therefore, that when discriminative knowledge is perfectly developed before the Prârabdha has worked itself out, the incarnate Puruṣa in question, is released, but remains awhile burdened with the Body. This is what is called Jîvan-Mukti or the state of release during life.

When a Jîvan-Mukta is finally released.

प्राप्ते शरीरभेदे चरितार्थत्वात् प्रधानविनिवृत्तौ ।
ऐकान्तिकमात्यन्तिकमुभयं कैवल्यमाप्नोति ॥ ६८ ॥

प्राप्ते Prâpte, come to pass, that is, on the exhaustion of Prârabdha Karma by experience. शरीरभेदे Śarîra-bhede, on separation from the body. चरितार्थत्वात् Charita-artha-tvât, for the reason that she has fulfilled her purpose, *viz.*, Creation for the experience and release of Puruṣa. प्रधानविनिवृत्तौ Pradhâna-vinivṛittau, on the cessation of the activity of the Pradhâna. ऐकान्तिकम् Aikântikam, certain, absolute. आत्यन्तिकम् Âtyantikam, final, imperishable. उभयं Ubhayaṃ, both. कैवल्यम् Kaivalyam, singleness, pureness, freedom from the reflection of the threefold pain. आप्नोति Âpnoti, attains.

LXVIII. When (in due course) separation from the Body takes place, and there is cessation of the activity of the Pradhâna from her purpose having been fulfilled Puruṣa attains both absolute and final Kaivalya.

Origin of the Sâṃkhya declared.

पुरुषार्थज्ञानमिदं गुह्यं परमर्षिणा समाख्यातम्।
स्थित्युत्पत्तिप्रलयाश्चिन्त्यन्ते यत्र भूतानाम् ॥ ६९ ॥

पुरुषार्थज्ञानम् Puruṣa-artha-jñânam, knowledge for the accomplishment of the end of Puruṣa, *i.e.*, release. इदं Idaṃ, this. गुह्यं Guhyaṃ, secret, abstruse, unintelligible to the dull. परमर्षिणा Parama-ṛiṣiṇâ, by the great Ṛiṣi or Seer, namely Kapila. समाख्यातम् Sam-âkhyâtam, thoroughly expounded, expounded in all details. स्थित्युत्पत्तिप्रलयाः Sthiti-utpatti-pralayâḥ, duration, production, and dissolution. चिन्त्यन्ते Chintyante, are considered, discussed. यत्र Yatra, wherein. भूतानाम् Bhûtânâm, of created things, beings.

LXIX. This abstruse knowledge, adapted to the end of Puruṣa, wherein the production, duration, and dissolution of beings are considered, has been thoroughly expounded by the great Ṛiṣi.

ANNOTATION.

77. Vâchaspati construes the second line of the Kârikâ in a different manner. It is thus : Yatra, wherein, that is, in which knowledge, that is to say, for which knowledge, the origin, duration and destruction of living beings are considered by the Śrutis. Hereby he wants to bring out the sense that the Sâṃkhya is connected with, and is supported by, the Veda.

Traditional succession of the Sâṃkhya stated.

एतत् पवित्रमग्र्यं मुनिरासुरयेऽनुकम्पया प्रददौ।
आसुरिरपि पञ्चशिखाय तेन च बहुधाकृतं तन्त्रम् ॥७०॥

एतत् Etat, this. पवित्रम् Pavitram, purifying, *i.e.*, from the sin causing the threefold pain. अग्र्यं Agryaṃ, first in order, principal among all purifying things, foremost. मुनिः Muniḥ, Muni, sage Kapila. आसुरये Âsuraye, to Âsuri. अनुकम्पया Anukampayâ, through compassion. प्रददौ Pradadau, taught, imparted. आसुरिः Âsuriḥ, Âsuri. अपि Api, again. पञ्चशिखाय Pañchaśikhâya, to Pañchaśikha. तेन Tena, by him. च Cha, and. बहुधाकृतं Bahu-dhâ-kṛitaṃ, extensively propagated, elaborated in manifold ways. तन्त्रम् Tantram, the system.

LXX. This foremost purifying knowledge the Muni, through compassion, imparted to Asuri ; Âsuri, again, to Pañchaśikha, by whom the System was elaborated in manifold ways.

ANNOTATION.

78. In this and the succeeding Kârikâ the traditional succession of the Sâṃkhya doctrine is recorded with a view to establish its authentic character and thereby to inspire reverence towards it.

79. According to Gauḍapâda, the Sâṃkhya-Kârikâ ends with this Kârikâ. "For the Sâṃkhya which is the cause of release from transmigration, was declared by the Muni Kapila, wherein or in regard to which," as he says, "there are these seventy verses in the Âryâ metre." This is supported by the other traditional name for the Sâṃkhya-Kârikâ, which is Sâṃkhya-Saptati or the Seventy (Verses) on the Sâṃkhya. Vâchaspati, on the other hand, has not questioned the genuineness, or the claim to authority, of the additional two Kârikâs and has added his comment to them.

Above continued.

शिष्यपरम्परयागतमीश्वरकृष्णेन स चैतदार्याभिः ।
संक्षिप्तमार्यमतिना सम्यग् विज्ञाय सिद्धान्तम् ॥ ७१ ॥

शिष्यपरम्परया Śiṣya-paramparayâ, by tradition of disciples. आगतम् Âgatam, descended, received. ईश्वरकृष्णेन Îśvarakriṣṇena, by Îśvarakriṣṇa, the author of the Sâṃkhya-Kârikâ. सः Saḥ, this. च Cha, and. एतत्, this. आर्याभिः Âryâbhiḥ, by Ârya verses. संक्षिप्तम् Saṃkṣiptam, abridged, summarised, compendiously written. आर्यमतिना Ârya-matinâ, whose intelligence reached to the Tattvas; holy-minded. सम्यक् Samyak, thoroughly. विज्ञाय Vijñâya, understanding, realising. सिद्धान्तम् Siddhântam, domonstrated truth, established tenet, doctrine.

LXXI. And this doctrine, descended by tradition of disciples, to the holy-minded Iśvarakriṣṇa, having been thoroughly understood by him, has been summarised by means of these Âryâs.

Relation of the Sâṃkhya-Kârikâ to the Sâṃkya-Pravachana-Sûtram.

सप्तत्यां किल येऽर्थास्तेऽर्थाः कृत्स्नस्य षष्टितन्त्रस्य ।
आख्यायिकाविरहिताः परवादविवर्जिताश्चापि ॥ ७२ ॥

सप्तत्या Saptatyâ, by the seventy-versed treatise. किल Kila, truly. ये Ye, what. अर्थाः Arthâḥ, subjects, topics. ते Te, those. अर्थाः Arthâḥ, subjects. कृत्स्नस्य Kritsna-sya, entire, whole. षष्टितन्त्रस्य Ṣaṣṭi-tantra-sya, of the system of sixty topics. आख्यायिकाविरहिताः Âkhyâyikâ-virahitâḥ, disjoined from the illustrative stories. परवादविवर्जिताः Para-vâda-vivarjitâḥ, omitting demolition of opposite doctrines. च Cha, and. अपि Api, also.

LXXII. The subjects which are treated by the Saptati, are the subjects of the entire Ṣaṣṭi-Tantra, exclusive of the illustrative stories, and omitting demolition of opposite doctrines.

ANNOTATION.

80. The term Ṣaṣṭi-Tantra alludes to the Sâṃkhya-Pravachana-Sûtram divided into the six Books, namely, of Topics, of the Evolutions of the Pradhâna, of Dispassion, of Fables, of the Demolition of Counter-Theories, and of Recapitulation of Teachings. It is thus constructive, illustrative and destructive in its method. In its constructive portions, it establishes the sixty topics of the Sâṃkhya System. The same is done by the Saptati as well. Inasmuch, however, as the latter omits the stories and controversies, and also does not deal with the topics in so much detail, it has, in the preceding Kârikâ, been described as a summary of the former.

The sixty topics alluded to above are: 1. the existence, that is, conjunction with, and disjunction from, Puruṣa, of the Pradhâna, 2. her unity or singleness, 3. her objectiveness, 4. her subservience, 5. the distinctness of Puruṣa, 6. his manifoldness, 7. his inactivity, 8. his conjunction, 9. his disjunction, and 10. the duration of the rest,—these are the ten radical topics.

According to another enumeration, the ten radical categories are 1. Puruṣa, 2. Prakṛiti, 3. Mahat, 4. Ahamkâra, 5-7. Sattva, Rajas, and Tamas, 8. the Tan-Mâtras, 9. the Indriyas, and 10. the Elements.

A third enumeration specifies them as, 1. the eternality of Puruṣa and Prakṛiti, 2. the reality of experience and discriminative knowledge in Prakṛiti, 3. the unity of Prakṛiti and of Puruṣa, throughout transmigration, 4. the subservience of Prakṛiti, 5. the difference between Puruṣa and Prakṛiti, 6. the inactivity of Paruṣa, 7. the multiplicity of Puruṣa, 8. the conjunction of Puruṣa and Prakṛiti at the time of creation, 9. the disjunction of Puruṣa and Prakṛiti at the time of release, and 10. the pre-existence of Mahat and the other Tattvas in their respective causes.

Add to them, the five kinds of error, nine of complacency, twenty-eight of incapacity, and eight of perfection. Thus the number sixty is obtained.

Alphabetical Index of Karikas.

Words Index of the Karikas.

APPENDIX VII.

PANCHAŚIKHA SÛTRAM

OR

A FEW OF THE APHORISMS OF PANCHAŚIKHA.

PANCHASIKHA-SUTRAM.

INTRODUCTORY.

1. Páñchaśikha is one of the few earliest writers on the Sâṃkhya. He is an authority on the subject, and is mentioned as an Âchârya or Professor of the School. According to Îśvarakṛiṣṇa, the author of Sâṃkhya-Kârikâ, the original Sâṃkhya which descended from its founder Kapila to Pañchaśikha (through Âsuri, see Sâṃkhya-Kârikâ, No. LXX), was elaborated by him in manifold ways. But not a single one of his works is amongst the current coins of the Sâṃkhya literature. "He is known, by scanty fragments, as the author of a collection of philosophical aphorisms. One other performance, if not two, is likewise imputed to him; and he, perhaps, descanted on the theistic (sic) Sâṃkhya as well as on the atheistic (sic.)" (F. E. Hall). It would appear, from Vijñâna Bhikṣu's Commentary on the Vedânta-Sûtram, that Pañchaśikha wrote a commentary on the Tattva-Samâsa.

2. The only source, as yet discovered, so far as we know, from which a few of the aphorisms of Pañchaśikha can be recovered, is Vyâsa's Commentary on the Yoga-Sûtram of Patañjali. In the Preface to his edition of the Sâṃkhya-Pravachana-Bhâṣyam of Vijñâna Bhikṣu, Mr. Fitz-Edward Hall has collected eleven aphorisms of Pañchaśikha quoted by Vyâsa in his said Commentary. Another collection of extracts from the same source has been published, under the title of Pañchaśikha-âchârya-praṇîta Sâṃkhya-Sûtra, by Paṇḍita Râjâ Ram, Professor of Sanskrit, D. A. V. College, Lahore, in Nos. 4 and 5, Vol. VIII, 1912, of the series entitled Ârṣa-Granthâvali, Lahore. This collection contains twenty-one aphorisms including one of Vârṣagaṇya. Quite recently, again, we had a peculiar opportunity of examining the MS. of another collection of aphorisms attributed to Pañchaśikha, prepared by Svâmî Hariharânanda Araṇya of the Kâpila Âśrama in the District of Hooghli. This was obviously not an original compilation, but a reproduction of the Lahore publication, with a few additions, one of which was taken from the Veda without acknowledgment! As regards the collection of Mr. Fitz-Edward Hall and the collection of Paṇḍita Râja Râm, we have found that the one is, in certain respects, more complete and correct than the other, while the paternity of some of the aphorisms attributed in it to Pañchaśikha

is not free from suspicion. These will be noticed more in detail in the subsequent pages.

3. "Little can safely be conjectured," as rightly observes Mr. Fitz-Edward Hall, "with regard to the character of the work or works from which these sentences were collected by Vyâsa. They may be text; and they may be commentary. Probably they are Sâṃkhya; but, possibly, they pertain to the Yoga. That Pañchaśikha treated of other subjects than the Sâṃkhya, may be inferred from a remark of Vijñāna Bhikṣu's:

Svaprayojana-abhâve'pi viduṣâṃ pravṛittau Pañchaśikha-âchârya-vâkyaṃ sâṃkhya-sthaṃ pramâṇayati.—Yoga-Vârtika, I. 25."

आदिविद्वान् निर्माणचित्तमधिष्ठाय कारुण्याद्भगवान् परमर्षिरासुरये जिज्ञासमानाय तन्त्रं प्रोवाच ॥

4. आदिविद्वान् Âdi-Vidvân, the primeval Seer. "Primeval" means produced at the beginning of Creation. "Seer" means Darśana-kâra or one who has had direct vision of Puruṣa, as distinct from Prakṛiti. In its primary significance, the term "Âdi-Vidvân" is applicable to Viṣṇu alone. Here it refers to Kapila, the reputed founder of the Sâṃkhya Tantra, because "it is the self-existent Viṣṇu who appeared as the first Wise Man, Kapila, at the beginning of the current cycle of Cosmic Evolution, endowed with virtue, knowledge, dispassion, and infallible will" (Vâchaspati Miśra).

5. निर्माणचित्तमधिष्ठाय Nirmâṇa-chittam adhiṣṭhâya, presiding over, ensouling, or through the medium of, a self-made mental vehicle. These words explain how Viṣṇu became incarnated as Kapila. He, by an act of will, reproduced Himself as the mighty sage Kapila. Kapila was not a developed man, but an enveloped Divinity. This artificial creation of bodies, ensouled by artificial emanations of the mind, which is one of the most wonderful discoveries of the Hindu Spiritual Science, is not expected to make any deep impression on the minds of the majority of Western Scholars in the present age, nor to engage them in the investigation or in an examination of the truth in this matter, in a true scientific spirit. Neither do we here propose to enter into a discussion with them on this subject. We shall simply mention, for the information of readers at large, that this subject of the creation of artificial bodies and minds is dealt with in the Yoga-Sûtram of Patañjali, IV. 4, 5, and 6 (See the Sacred Books of the Hindus, Vol IV., 272-273). And to make the words of our text a little more illuminating to them, we may take the following extract from the Introduction to the above volume :—

"A Yogî, having attained the power of Samâdhi, sets about destroying his past Karmas. All Karmas may be divided into three classes :—(1) The acts done in the past, the consequences of which the man *must* suffer in the present life; the Karmas to expiate which he has taken the present birth or incarnation. They are the *ripe* Karmas (Prârabdha). (2) The Karmas done in the past, but which are not ripe, and will have to be expiated in some future life. They are the *stored* Karmas, or *unripe* (Sañchita). (3) The Karmas which a man creates in his present life, and which have to be expiated in a future or the present life. This last kind of act,—the fresh Karmas, can be stopped. By devotion to the Lord and doing everything in a spirit of service, no *fresh* Karmas are generated. The incurring of debt is stopped. The man, however, has to pay off past debts—the ripe and unripe Karmas. The ripe Karmas will produce their effects in the present life. The Yogî does not trouble himself about this. But the *unripe* or *stored* Karmas require a future birth. It is here that the Yoga is of the greatest practical importance. The Yogî is not bound to wait for future lives in order to get an opportunity to pay off the debt of Sañchita Karmas. He simultaneously *creates* ALL the bodies that those Sañchita Karmas require,—through those bodies expiates all his Karmas simultaneously. Every one of such bodies has a Chitta or mentality of his own. This is the Nirmâṇa-chitta or the Artificial mind—like the Pseudo-Personalities of hypnoptic trance. These artificial minds arise simultaneously like so many sparks from the Âhaṃkâric matter of the Yogî's Self, and they ensoul the artificial bodies created for them. These artificial bodies, with artificial minds in them, walk through the earth in hundreds,—they are distinguished from ordinary men by the fact that they are perfectly methodical in all their acts, and automatic in their lives. All these artificials are controlled by the consciousness of the Yogî,—one consciousness controlling hundred automatons. Every one of these automatons has a particular destiny, a particular portion of the Sañchita Karma to exhaust. As soon as that destiny is fulfilled, the Yogî withdraws his ray from it, and the " man " dies a sudden death,—a heart-failure generally.

" Now, what is the difference between the ordinary mind and the Yoga-created mind,—the natural Chitta and the artificial Chitta? The natural mind by experience gains a habit, the impressions are stored in it, and they, as Vâsanâs, become the seeds of desires and activities. The artificial mind is incapable of storing up impressions in it. It has no Vâsanâs and consequently it disintegrates as soon as the body falls down."

6. कारुण्यात् Kâruṇyât, through compassion. This word, according to Vyâsa, tells us what the teaching of the text is. It is this that Îśvara, out of the abundance of His compassion towards all Puruṣas, incarnates Himself, from time to time, in order to teach them knowledge and virtue, whereby they may be delivered from bondage. The passage of the text is quoted by Vyâsa in his Commentary on the Yoga-Sûtram, I. 25, and Vâchaspati explains the purpose of the quotation thus: "This theory that the compassionate Lord teaches knowledge and virtue is also common to the teaching of Kapila:—So has it been said by Pañchaśikha." *Râma Prasâda's translation.*

7. भगवान् Bhagavân, divine. This term connotes the possession of

virtue, knowledge, dispassion, and infallible will. And we know that these were cognate with Kapila.

8. परमर्षि: Parama-ṛiṣiḥ, the mighty sage. Viṣṇu appeared on earth as Kapila, in the highly purified and richly developed body of a saint who held communion with the gods. The necessity for such bodies for divine manifestations has been admirably explained and illustrated by the late Babu Sisir Kumar Ghosh in his *Lord Gaurâñga.*

9. आसुरये Âsuraye, to Âsuri, a disciple of Kapila and the first recipient of the Sâṃkhya.

10. जिज्ञासमानाय Jijñâsamânâya, who wished to know Âsuri approached the divine man Kapila and desired to know from him the means for the accomplishment of the Supreme Good, namely, the permanent prevention of pain.

11. तन्त्रं Tantraṃ, the systematic teaching, the Sâṃkhya doctrine.

12. प्रोवाच Pra-uvâcha, declared fully, revealed. Such, then, is the origin of the Sâṃkhya.

I. The primeval Seer, (incarnated), through the medium of an artificial mind, (as) the mighty divine sage (Kapila), out of compassion (towards all entangled Puruṣas), revealed the (Sâṃkhya) doctrine, in a systematic way, to Âsuri, who desired to know them.

13. Now, what is this Sâṃkhya Darśana? "Darśana" etymologically means the act or the result of seeing, from the root √Dṛiś, to see. Here it stands for Sâkṣâtkâra or immeditae vision, that is, intuition of the Self. And "Sâṃkhya" means that by which something is perfectly revealed, from the root √Khyâ, to manifest. The "Sâṃkhya Darśana," therefore, is that form of Spiritual Intuition of the Self, whereby the nature of the Self is perfectly revealed. So declares Pañchaśikha :—

एकमेव दर्शनं ख्यातिरेव दर्शनम् ॥

एकम् Ekam, one, single. एव Eva, only, there is no second. दर्शनं Darśanaṃ, intuition, knowledge. ख्याति : Khyâtiḥ, coming to light, shining, manifestation, illumination. एव Eva, alone. दर्शनम् Darśanam, intuition, knowledge.

II. There is but one Spiritual Intuition of the Self; it is nothing but manifestation which is the Spiritual Intuition of the Self.

14. The word 'Khyâti' is suggestive in more respects than one. Now, manifestation is declared to be the means of accomplishing Mokṣa or Release. (1) What, then, must be its nature? It cannot obviously be of the nature of the attainment of some advanced state or development from a state less advanced or less developed; for Manifestation itself cannot accomplish this. It will also be repugnant to the Sâṃkhya conception of the Self; for the Self is kûṭastha, unchangeable; it ever *is*, never *becomes*. It follows, therefore, that Mokṣa consists merely in the removal of a shadow, as it were, that is, of something which casts its reflection on the Self and thereby overshadows it and causes obstruction to its shining out in the fullness of its own light. (2) This shadow, this obstruction, is not of, or from, the Self, but is a creation of the Not-Self. And what is the cause of its origin, the same is also the cause of its removal. It fades or deepens, it contracts or expands, it exists or ceases to exist, and for this depends entirely on the activity or non-activity of the Not-Self. (3) The Self is altogether passive and inert. Shadow or no shadow, it is ever there, all-full, ever shining, unaffected, unsullied. In ignorance, men speak of the Bondage of the Self which is never bound, ever released. Bondage, in reality, is this supreme ignorance, this veil of the Not-Self,—the non-discrimination of the principle of Becoming and the principle of Being,—to which alone is due all the suffering in the world,—not exactly suffering, for actual suffering there can be, and is, nothing in the Self, but the Abhimâna or assumption or attribution of it to the Self. Replace non-discrimination by Discrimination, the veil is gone, and gone with it is the Shadow—the obstruction—and see the ever pure, ever constant, ever shining Self.

15. This Aphorism of Pañchaśikha has been quoted by Vyâsa in his Commentary on the Aphorism I. 4 of Patañjali's Yoga-Sûtram in the following context: Yoga is the inihibition of the modifications of the mind (chitta) (Yoga-Sûtram I: 2). Then the Seer (Puruṣa) stands in his own nature (*Ibid* I. 3), that is, is established in his own intrinsic form, as in the state of kaivalya or absolute abstractedness. Elsewhere (there takes place in him) similarity of form with the modifications (*Ibid* I. 4). How does it take place? Because objects are presented to him. Whatever, therefore, be the modifications of the mind, with the same is Puruṣa invested, so long as the mind remains up and doing. That is to say, Puruṣa, with the light of his intelligence, illuminates the manifold modifications of the active mind, which, consequently, are mistaken as being the manifestations of Puruṣa. It is thus this mistake, the failure to distinguish between the unintelligent modifications of

the unintelligent mind and the intelligence of the inert, immutable Puruṣa, which is the cause of all the mental phenomena so universally attributed to Puruṣa. In reality, however, the manifestation of Puruṣa is one and one only, the same at all times and in all circumstances. And so there is the Aphorism : "There is but one Spiritual Intuition of the Self ; it is nothing but Manifestation, which is the Spiritual Intuition of the Self."

16. The Self is most difficult to know. It is inscrutable. Only a steady, pure, and peaceful mind can reflect it as it is in itself. Steadiness of the mind implies a long and arduous process of Yogic practice. The stepping-stone to it is what is called Jyotiṣmatî or the state of lucidity, or the activity which causes illumination. This activity of the mind is twofold, according as it is painless objective (viśoka-viṣayavatî) or is purely egoistic (asmitâ-mâtrâ). It is described by Vyâsa in his Commentary on Yoga-Sûtram, I. 36, in the following manner: "It is the consciousness of thought-forms (Buddhi), on the part of one who practises concentration upon the Lotus of the Heart. For, the substance of Buddhi is refulgent and is like Âkâśa, *i.e.*, all-pervading. Through success in concentration upon that, the activity of the mind modifies by the forms having the colour of the light of the sun, the moon, the planets and precious stones. Likewise, the mind concentrated upon Asmitâ, I-aṃ-ness or egoism, becomes pure egoism, calm and infinite, like a waveless ocean." And he supports his exposition by quoting the following Aphorism of Pañchaśikha:

तमणुमात्रमात्मानुविद्यास्मीत्येवं तावत् संप्रजानीते ॥

तम् Tam, that. अणुमात्रम् Aṇu-mâtram, of the size of an atom, small as an atom, difficult to understand, inscrutable. आत्मानम् Âtmânam, Self. अनुविद्य Anu-vidya, knowing at last. अस्मि Asmi, am. इति Iti, that. एवं Evaṃ, in this form. तावत् Tâvat, for certain. संप्रजानीते Saṃ-pra-jânîte, fully and accurately knows.

III. Knowing, at last, that inscrutable Self, his consciousness mainfests as "I am" only.

17. It has been mentioned above that the identification of the Principle of Being with the Principle of Becoming, of the Self with the Not-Self, is the cause of all the suffering in the Universe. This identification is called A-vidyâ. Its nature is declared by Pañchaśikha in the following two Aphorisms :

व्यक्तमव्यक्तं वा सत्त्वमात्मत्वेनाभिप्रतीत्य तस्य संपदमनुनन्दत्यात्मसंपदं मन्वानस्तस्य व्यापदमनुशोचत्यात्मव्यापदं मन्वानः स सर्वोऽप्रतिबुद्धः ॥

व्यक्तम् Vyaktam, unfolded, sentient substances or existences. such as wife, son, animals, etc. अव्यक्तं A-vyaktaṃ, not unfolded, insentient objects, such as riches, house, couch, etc. वा Vâ, or. सत्त्वम् Sattvam, existence, substance, object. आत्मत्वेन Âtma-tvena, under the characteristic of the Self, as being the Self. अभिप्रतीत्य Abhi-pratîtya, approaching towards in mind, thinking, believing, taking up. तस्य Tasya, its, of the object. संपदम् Saṃpadam, prosperity, well-being. अनुनन्दति Anu-nandati, rejoices at or according to. आत्मसंपदं Âtma-Saṃpadaṃ, well-being of the Self. मन्वानः Manvânaḥ, imagining. तस्य Tasya, its, of the object. व्यापदम् Vyâpa-dam, adversity. अनुशोचति Anu-Sochati, grieves according to. आत्मव्यापदं Âtma-vyâpa-daṃ, adversity of the Self. मन्वानः Manvânaḥ, imagining. सः Saḥ, he. सर्वः Sarvaḥ, all. अप्रतिबुद्धः A-prati-buddhaḥ, unawakened in regard to the truth.

IV. They are all unawakened who, believing the objective entities, whether they be sentient or insentient, to be the Self, rejoice at their prosperity, imagining it to be the prosperity of the Self, and grieve at their adversity, imagining it to be the adversity of the Self.

18. This Aphorism has been quoted by Vyâsa in his Commentary on Yoga-Sûtram II. 5 which describes A-vidyâ as being "the manifestation of the non-eternal, the impure, the painful, and the Not-Self to be the eternal, the pure, the pleasant, and the Self."

बुद्धितः परं पुरुषमाकारशीलविद्यादिभिरपश्यन् कुर्यात्तत्रात्म-बुद्धि मोहेन ॥

बुद्धितः Buddhi-taḥ, from Buddhi. परं Paraṃ, different. पुरुषम् Puruṣam, Puruṣa. आकारशीलविद्यादिभिः Âkâra-Sîla-vidyâ-âdibhiḥ, by nature, character, knowledge, etc. The nature of Puruṣa is constant purity. Indifference is his character. By knowledge is denoted his being intelligent. Whereas Buddhi is impure, not indifferent, and non-intelligent. अपश्यन् A-paśyan, not seeing. कुर्यात् Kuryât, is led to form. तत्र Tatra, therein, in respect of Buddhi. आत्मबुद्धिं Âtma-buddhiṃ, the notion of the Self. मोहेन Mohena, by reason of the dullness (of Tamas).

V. Not knowing Puruṣa to be different from Buddhi in nature, character, knowledge, etc., a man is led, by reason of the dullness born of Tamas, to form the notion of the Self in respect of Buddhi.

19. The above has been quoted by Vyâsa in his Commentary on the Yoga-Sûtram II. 6 which describes Asmitâ or Egoism as being "the apparent identity of the subjective power of seeing (*i.e.*, Puruṣa) and the instrumental power of seeing (*i. e.*, Buddhi)."

20. It follows, therefore, that there is Bondage as long as this notion of the Self in respect of the Not-Self remains, and that there is Release when this notion is destroyed by the knowledge of the Self as being distinct and different from the Not-Self in all essential particulars.

स्यात् स्वल्पः संकरः सपरिहारः सप्रत्यवमर्शः कुशलस्य नापकर्षायालम् ॥

स्यात् Syât, can be. स्वल्पः Svalpaḥ, little. संकरः Samkaraḥ, mixture. सपरिहारः Sa-parihâraḥ attended with, *i.e.*, capable of, avoidance or removal. सप्रत्यवमर्शः Sa-pratiavamarśaḥ, attended with, *i.e.*, capable of, being borne easily. कुशलस्य Kuśalasya, of the good. न Na, not. अपकर्षाय Apakarṣâya, for damage or impairment or lessening the effect. अलम् Alam, sufficient, strong or powerful enough.

VI. A little mixture (of evil entailed, for instance, by the killing of animals) which is capable of removal (by expiation) or is easy to bear, cannot prevail for the diminution of the (greater) good (produced by the performance of sacrifices such as the Aśvamedha and the like).

21. The above bears reference to the vexed question as to the consequences of the acts of sin necessarily committed in the course of the performance of sacrifices which are calculated to produce merits of far-reaching consequences. For instance, an Aśvamedha sacrifice cannot be performed without the killing of a horse, and killing is a sinful act. So that, while the performance of the Aśvamedha produces its desirable consequences, the killing of the horse cannot, at the same time, fail to produce its undesirable consequences. The question, therefore, arises whether what is acquired through the sacrifice, be not lost through the sin. This is an important issue arising in the discussion of the Law of Karma as a whole.

22. Now, "the killing of animals, etc., has," as Vâchaspati explains, "two effects. The first is that, being ordained as part of the principal action, it helps in its fulfilment. The second is that, the causing of pain to all living beings being forbidden, it results in undesirable consequences. Of these, when it is performed only as subsidiary to the principal action, then, for that very reason, it does not manifest its result all at once, independently of the principal action. On the contrary, it keeps its position of an accessory only, and manifests only when the fruition of the principal ruling action begins. It is said to be tacked on to the ruling action, when, while helping the ruling action, it exists as the seed of its own proper effect. Pañchaśikha has said the following on the subject: A, little mixture.'

"When the ruling factor of the present karma, born from the sacrifice of Jyotiṣṭoma, etc , is mixed up with the present cause of evil, it may be easily removed. It is possible of removal by a small expiatory sacrifice. Even if an expiatory sacrifice be not performed by carelessness, the subsidiary action would ripen at the time of the ripening of the principal only, and, in that case, the evil generated thereby would be easy to bear. The wise who are taking their baths in the great lake of the nectar of pleasure brought about by a collection of good actions, put up easily with a small piece of the fire of pain produced by a small evil. It is not, therefore, capable of diminishing, *i.e.*, appreciably lessening the effect of the good, *i.e.*, of his large virtues."—*Râma Prasâda's translation.*

23. This Aphorism of Pañchaśikha has been quoted by Vyâsa in his Commentary on the Yoga-Sûtram II. 13. "So long as the cause remains, the fruition of Merit and Demerit is in the kind of birth, length of life and experience."

24. Pandit Raja Ram is wrong in reading the next sentence in the Commentary as part of the present Aphorism. For both Svapneśvara and Vâchaspati are against this reading.

25. But the fact remains that even a highly meritorious act is tainted with sin, and with consequent pain. It is even as Patañjali declares that "to the discriminative, all is pain" (Yoga-Sûtram II. 15). And pain is the thing which every mortal seeks to get rid of: not merely present pain, but pain not-yet-come is the thing to be avoided (Yoga-Sûtram II. 16). Accordingly, both in the Sâṃkhya and in the Yoga Śâstra, enquiries have been instituted into the cause of its origin as well as into the means of its removal. In the Yoga-Sûtram II. 17, Patañjali declares that the conjunction of Buddhi and Puruṣa is the cause of pain. And on this subject, also says Pañchaśikha :

तत्संयोगहेतुविवर्जनात् स्यादयमात्यन्तिको दुःखप्रतीकारः ॥

तत्संयोगहेतुविवर्जनात् Tat-Saṃyoga-hetu-vivarjanât, through abandonment of the cause, namely, Non-discrimination, of the conjunction thereof, *i.e.*, of Buddhi. स्यात् Syât, will be. अयम् Ayam, this, *i.e.*, the desired prevention of pain not-yet-come. आत्यन्तिकः Âtyantikaḥ, final, permanent. दुःखप्रतीकारः Duḥkha-pratîkâraḥ, prevention or remedy of pain.

VII. Through the abandonment of the cause thereof, there can be the permanent prevention of pain, which is desired.

26. The above has been quoted by Vyâsa in his Commentary on the Yoga-Sûtram II. 17.

27. Pain is due to conjunction. Rajas gives rise to pain in Sattva, which reflects it on Puruṣa, through conjunction. In this reflection consists the experience (Bhoga) of Puruṣa from which emancipation (Apavarga is sought. To describe them more correctly, Bhoga is the ascertainment of the essential nature of the Guṇas, as desirable and undesirable, in their undifferentiated form ; and Apavarga is the ascertainment of the essential nature of the Experiencer, through the withdrawal of the influence of Prakṛiti upon him. To accomplish both these objects, namely, Bhoga and Apavarga, is the creation of the world. Creation is the exhibition of Prakṛiti to Puruṣa. Puruṣa regards or looks at Prakṛiti from these points of view only ; and there is no third point of view. So declares Pañchaśikha also :

अयंतु खलु त्रिषु गुणेषु कर्तृष्वकर्तरि च पुरुषे तुल्यातुल्यजातीये तत्क्रियासाक्षिण्युपनीयमानान्त्सर्वभावाननुपश्यन्नदर्शनमन्यच्छंकते ॥

अयं Ayam, this Puruṣa. तु Tu, but. खलु Khalu, surely. त्रिषु Triṣu, in the three. गुणेषु Guṇeṣu, in the Guṇas, Sattva, Rajas, and Tamas. कर्तृषु Kartṛiṣu, which are the actors, agents. अकर्तरि A Kartari, who is not the actor. च Cha, and. पुरुषे Puruṣe, in Puruṣa. तुल्यातुल्यजातीये Tulya-a-tulya-jâtîye, who is of a like and unlike kind. चतुर्थे Chaturthe, the fourth. तत्क्रियासाक्षिणि Tat-kriyâ-sâkṣiṇi, who is the witness of the action thereof, *i.e.*, of the Guṇas. उपनीयमानान् Upanîyamânân, that are being presented. सर्वभावान् Sarva-bhâvân, all objects. उपपन्नान् Upapannân, established, known. अनुपश्यन् Anupaśyan, knowing. न Na, not. दर्शनम् Darśanam, view. अन्यत् Anyat, other. शंकते Śaṅkate, suspects.

VIII. This one, however, seeing all things explained as these are being presented to the three Guṇas as the actors and to the fourth, *viz.*, Puruṣa, of a like and unlike kind, as the non-actor and as the witness of their action, does not suspect (the existence of) any other point of view, or object of knowledge.

28. "Of a like and unlike kind":—For instance, the Guṇas are eternal, so is Puruṣa ; Puruṣa is intelligent, but the Guṇas are non-intelligent.

29. "The above has been quoted by Vyâsa in his Commentary on Yoga-Sûtram II 18 : The object (Dṛiśya) which possesses the nature of illumination (Sattva), activity (Rajas), and inertia (Tamas) and consists

of the elements and of the powers of cognition and action, exists for the purpose of experience and of emancipation.

30. "But these two, experience and emancipation, which are effected by Buddhi, reside in Buddhi alone; how are they, then," asks Vyasa, "predicated of Puruṣa?" He next gives the answer: "Just as victory or defeat, which lies in the army, is predicated of the owner of the army, as he is the experiencer of its consequences, so too are Bondage and Release, residing in Buddhi alone, are predicated of Puruṣa, as he is the experiencer of their consequences. Of Buddhi alone are Bondage in the shape of the non-accomplishment of the object of Puruṣa, and Release in the shape of the fulfilment thereof. Similarly, are perception, memory, reasoning, doubt, knowledge of the truth, and blind attachment to life, which reside in Buddhi, are attributed as existing in Puruṣa, as he is the experiencer of their consequences, by having their reflections thrown upon him from Buddhi, through proximity."

31. Puruṣa, then, is neither quite similar to Buddhi nor quite dissimilar to it. He is not quite subject to Bondage and Release, nor is quite free from them. On this subject, Pañchaśikha further declares:

अपरिणामिनी हि भोक्तृशक्तिरप्रतिसंक्रमा च परिणामिन्यर्थे प्रतिसंक्रान्तेव तद्वृत्तिमनुपतति। तस्याश्च प्राप्तचैतन्योपग्रहरूपाया बुद्धिवृत्तेरनुकारमात्रतया बुद्धिवृत्त्याऽविशिष्टा हि ज्ञानवृत्तिरित्याख्यायते ॥

अपरिणामिनी A-pariṇâminî, not subject to transformation, unchangeable. हि Hi, for. भोक्तृशक्तिः Bhoktṛi-Śaktiḥ, the power of the experiencer, intelligence, consciousness. अप्रतिसंक्रमा A-prati-Saṇkramâ, not moving towards objects, inert, actionless, inactive. च Cha, and. परिणामिनी Pariṇâminî, subject to transformation, changeful. अर्थे Arthe, into the object, *i.e.*, Buddhi. प्रतिसंक्रान्ता Pratisaṃkrântâ, transferred, moved to. इव Iva, as if. तद्वृत्तिम् Tat-vṛittim, the modifications thereof, *i.e.*, of Buddhi. अनुपतति Anu-patati, imitates, modifies according to. तस्याः Tasyâḥ, its, *i.e.*, of Buddhi. च Cha, and. प्राप्तचैतन्योपग्रहरूपायाः Prâpta-chaitanya-upagraha-rûpâyâḥ, transformed by receiving the reflection of intelligence. बुद्धिवृत्तेः Bûddhi-vṛitteḥ, of the modification of Buddhi. अनुकारमात्रतया Anu-kâra-mâtra-tayâ, by reason of mere imitation. बुद्धिवृत्त्या Buddhi-vṛittyâ, by the modification of Buddhi अविशिष्टा A-viśiṣṭâ, unqualified. हि Hi, verily. ज्ञानवृत्तिः Jñâna-vṛittiḥ, modification of consciousness. इति Iti, thus. आख्यायते Âkhyâyate, called, described.

IX. For the power of the Experiencer which is unchangeable as well as inert, as if running into the changeful object (*i.e.*, Buddhi), imitates its modifications. And by reason of the mere imitation of the modifications of Buddhi, while that is transformed by receiving the reflection of intelligence, it (the imitation) is described as the modification of intelligence unqualified by the modification of Buddhi.

32. The above has been quoted by Vyâsa in his Commentary on Yoga-Sûtram II. 20: "The seer is the power of seeing merely: though pure, he sees ideas by imitation," and he thereby supports the proposition that "though pure, he sees ideas by imitation; because he sees, by imitation, ideas belonging to Buddhi, and, though he is not of the same nature as Buddhi, as he sees by imitation, because he looks as if he were of the nature of Buddhi." This is further explained by Vâchaspati in the following manner:

"Although the moon is not, as a matter of fact, transferred into pure water, yet, inasmuch as its reflection passes into water, it is, as it were, transferred into it. So also, the power of consciousness, although not actually transferred into the Buddhi, yet is, as it were, transferred into it, because it is reflected into it. By that fact, consciousness becomes, as it were, of the very nature of the will-to-be (Buddhi). It accordingly follows the modifications of the will-to-be. This explains the words "by imitation." It is said, it cognises by imitation, as it cognises by following the modifications of the will-to-be."—*Ram Prasâda's translation.*

33. Conjunction has been stated to be the cause of Bhoga. The objective world owes its existence to it. But when, in the case of a Puruṣa whose objects have been fulfilled, the objective world no longer exists for him, it does not at the same time altogether vanish out of existence, because there are other Puruṣas whose Bhoga and Apavarga still remain to be accomplished. (*Vide* the Yoga-Sûtram II. 22). Thus is the continuity of creation established. Hereby is also established that, whereas the Subject and the Object exist from eternity, their conjunction must, in the form of a stream of successive conjunctions, be without beginning. On this subject there has been quoted by Vyâsa, in his Commentary on the above Yoga-Sûtram, the following Aphorism of Pañchaśikha:

धर्मिणामनादिसंयोगात् धर्ममात्राणामप्यनादिः संयोगः ॥

धर्मिणाम Dharmiṇâm, of the containers, that is, the Guṇas, Sattva, Rajas, and Tamas. अनादिसंयोगात् An-âdi-saṃyogât, because conjunction with Puruṣa is without beginning. धर्ममात्राणाम् Dharma-mâtrâṇâm, of all the contained, that is, the products

Mahat and the rest. अपि Api, also. अनादिः An-âdiḥ, without beginning. संयोगः Saṃyogaḥ, conjunction.

X. Because the conjunction of the Guṇas (with Puruṣa) is without beginning, the conjunction also of the products thereof, taken as a class, is without beginning.

34. "It is for this reason that, although the conjunction of one Puruṣa with one manifestation of the principle of Mahat has ceased to exist, the conjunction of another Puruṣa with another manifestation of the Mahat has not become a thing of the past."—*Ram Prasada's translation of Vâchaspati.*

35. In the Yoga-Sûtram III. 13, Patañjali declares: "By this are described the changes of characteristic (dharma), of secondary quality (lakṣaṇa), and of condition (avasthâ) in the objective and instrumental phenomena."—*Ram Prasada's translation.*

36. In the course of his Commentary on the above, Vyâsa observes: "The change of secondary quality is the moving of the characteristic along the paths of being (past, present, and future). The past characteristic joined to the past secondary quality, is not devoid of the future and the present secondary quality. Similarly, the present (characteristic) joined to the present secondary quality, is not devoid of the past and the future secondary quality. Similarly, the future (characteristic) joined to the future secondary quality, is not devoid of the present and past secondary qualities. For example, a man who is attached to one woman, does not hate all the others.

"Others find a fault in this change of secondary qualities They say that all the qualities being in simultaneous existence, their paths of being must be confused, (and thus overlapping one another, cannot be considered as distinct and different).

"This is thus met: That the characteristics do exist as such, requires no proof. When there is such a thing as a characteristic, the differences of the secondary qualities also must be posited. It is not only in the present time that the characteristic characterizes. If it were so, the mind would not possess the characteristic of attachment, seeing that attachment is not in manifestation at the time of anger.—Further, the three (peaceful, fearful, and dull) secondary qualities are not possible of existence in one individual simultaneously. They may, however, appear in succession, by virtue of the operation of their several (exciting) causes. Therefore, there is no confusion. For example, attachment being in the height of manifestation with reference to some object, it does not, for that reason, cease to exist with reference to all other objects. On the contrary, it is then ordinarily in existence with reference to them."—*Ram Prasada's translation.*

And in support of the above view, Vyâsa quotes the following Aphorism of Pañchaśikha:

रूपातिशयाः वृत्त्यतिशयाश्च विरुध्यन्ते सामान्यानि त्वतिशयैः सह प्रवर्तन्ते ॥

रूपातिशयाः Rûpa-atiśayâḥ, intensities of nature or characteristic. वृत्त्यतिशयाः Vṛitti-atiśayâḥ, intensities of function or manifestation. च cha, and. विरुध्यन्ते Virudhyante, are opposed. सामान्यानि Sâmânyâni, ordinary ones. तु Tu, but. अतिशयैः Atiśayaiḥ, with the intense ones. सह Saha, with. प्रवर्तन्ते Pravartante, co-exist, co-operate.

XI. Intensities of characteristic and intensities of manifestation are opposed to each other, but the ordinary ones co-exist with the intense ones.

37. This simple Aphorism of Pañchaśikha embodies the discovery of the important doctrine of the sub-conscious mind.

38. As to the relation between Âkâśa and the Power of Hearing, there is the following Aphorism of Pañchaśikha:

तुल्यदेशश्रवणानामेकदेशश्रुतित्वं सर्वेषां भवति ॥

तुल्यदेशश्रवणानाम् Tulya-deśa-śravaṇânâm, of those having their powers of hearing similarly located, that is, equally in Âkâśa or soniferous ether. एकदेशश्रुतित्वं Eka-deśa-śruti-tvaṃ, to have the power of hearing in the same situation. सर्वेषां Sarveṣâm, of all. भवति Bhavati, is.

XII. In the case of all, having their powers of hearing equally located in Akâśa, hearing takes place in the same situation.

39. The above has been quoted by Vyâsa in his Commentary on the Yoga-Sûtram III. 40: "By Saṃyama over the relation between Âkâśa and the power-of-hearing, comes the higher power hearing."

40. And Vâchaspati explains its sense and significance in the following manner: "This sense of hearing, then, having its origin in the principle of egoism, acts like iron, drawn as it is by sound originating and located in the mouth of the speaker, acting as loadstone, transforms them into its own modifications in sequence of the sounds of the speaker, and thus senses them. And it is for this reason that for every living

creature, the perception of sound in external space is, in the absence of defects, never void of authority. So says the quotation from Pañchaśikha: "To all those whose organs of hearing are similarly situated, the situation of hearing is the same." "All those" are Chaitras and others whose powers of hearing are similarly situated in space. The meaning is, that the powers of hearing of all are located in Âkâśa. Further, the Âkâśa in which the power of hearing is located, is born out of the Soniferous Tanmâtra, and has therefore the quality of sound inherent in itself. It is by this sound acting in unison, that it takes the sound of external solids, etc. Hence the hearing, *i.e.*, the sound, of all is of the same class.

"This, then, establishes that Âkâśa is the substratum of the power of hearing, and also possesses the quality of sound. And this sameness of the situation of sound is an indication of the existence of Âkâśa. That which is the substratum of the auditory power (Śruti) which manifests as sound of the same class, is Âkâśa."—*Ram Prasada's translation.*

41. In his Pañchaśikha—Âchârya-praṇîta Sâṃkhya-Sûtra, Paṇḍita Râja Râm includes the following quotations by Vyâsa:

प्रधानं स्थित्यैव वर्तमानं विकाराकरणादप्रधानं स्यात् तथा गत्यैव वर्तमानं विकारनित्वत्यादप्रधानं स्यात् उभयथा चास्य प्रवृत्तिः प्रधानव्यवहारं लभते नान्यथा कारणान्तरेष्वपि कल्पितेष्वेष समानश्चर्चः ॥

XIII. The Pradhâna, the material cause of all manifestation, would become what it is not, if it tended only to rest, because in that case there would not be any manifestation into phenomena; nor would it be what it is, if it were to remain in constant motion, because in that case, the phenomena would become eternal and never disappear. It is only when it tends to both these states, that it can be called the Pradhâna (the cause of manifestation), not otherwise. The same considerations apply to any other causes that might be imagined.—*Vide* Vyâsa's Commentary on Yoga-Sûtram II. 23.

मूर्तिव्यवधिजातिभेदाभावान्नास्ति मूलपृथक्त्वम् ॥

XIV. On account of the absence of the difference of form, intervening space and time, and genus, there is no separation in the Root (*i.e.*, the Pradhâna.)—*Vide* Vyâsa's Commentary on Yoga-Sûtram III. 52.

जलभूम्योः पारिणामिकं रसादिवैश्वरूप्यं स्थावरेषु दृष्टं तथा स्थावराणां जङ्गमेषु जङ्गमानां स्थावरेषु ॥

XV. All the diverse forms of juice, etc., caused by the transformation of earth and water, is seen in immobile objects; similarly of the immobile, in the mobile, and of the mobile, in the immobile.—*Vide* Vyâsa's Commentary on Yoga-Sûtram III. 14.

एकजातिसमन्वितानामेषां धर्ममात्रं व्यावृत्तिः ॥

XVI. Of these which possess the same genus, the differences are in (specific) properties only.—*Vide* Vyasa's Commentary on Yoga-Sûtram III. 43.

महामोहमयेनेन्द्रजालेन प्रकाशशीलं सत्त्वमावृत्य तदेवाकार्ये नियुङ्क्ते ॥

XVII. By the magic panorama of Mahâmoha (desire and ignorance), overshadowing the Sattva which is luminous by nature, the very same is employed in acts of vice.—*Vide* Vyâsa's Commentary on Yoga-Sûtram II. 52.

तपो न परं प्राणायामात्ततो विशुद्धिर्मलानां दीप्तिश्च ज्ञानस्य ॥

XVIII. There is no penance greater than Prâṇâyâma: whence are the purification from dirts and the brightness of knowledge.—*Vide* Vyâsa's Commentary on Yoga-Sûtram II. 52.

स्वभावं मुक्त्वा येषां पूर्वपक्षे रुचिर्भवति अरुचिश्च निर्णये भवति ॥

XIX. (In the case of those who do not possess the curiosity to know the nature of the Self), giving up, through faults (*i. e.*, demerits), the nature, there arises a liking for *primâ facie* contrary views, and dislike for the ascertainment of the truth.—*Vide* Vyâsa's Commentary on Yoga-Sûtram, IV 25.

स खल्वयं ब्राह्मणो यथा यथा व्रतानि बहूनि समादित्सते तथा तथा प्रमादकृतेभ्यो हिंसानिदानेभ्यो निवर्तमानस्तामेवावदातरूपामहिंसां करोति ॥

XX. As a Brâhmaṇa undertakes many a vow, one after another, he turns away successively from acts of injury due to inadvertence, and thereby makes the virtue of non-injury (ahiṃsâ) gradually purer and purer.—*Vide* Vyâsa's Commentary on Yoga-Sûtram II. 30.

ये चैते मैत्र्यादयो ध्यायिनां विहारास्ते बाह्यसाधननिरनुग्रहात्मानः प्रकृष्टं धर्ममभिनिर्वर्तयन्ति ॥

XXI. And what are these activities of the Dhyâyins, namely, friendliness (maitrî), etc., being, by nature, independent of external means, accomplish the highest virtue.—*Vide* Vyâsa's Commentary on Yoga-Sûtram IV. 10.

42. And to them, the Kâpila Âśrama reproduction adds :

प्रधानस्यात्मख्यापनार्था प्रवृत्तिः ॥

XXII. The activity of the Pradhâna is for the sake of the exhibition of herself.—*Vide* Vyâsa's Commentary on Yoga-Sûtram II. 23.

43. But Vâchaspati tells us that No. XIII is a doctrine of an opposite school, and Nos. XVII—XX are the teachings of the Âgamins (Śaiva Darśana) ; while Vyâsa himself tells us that No. XIV is an aphorism of Vârṣagaṇya and No. XXII is a text of the Veda. Both of them, again, are silent as to the paternity of Nos. XV and XVI. The remaining one, No. XI, is referred by Vâchaspati to the Âchâryas or older teachers of the Sâṃkhya School. In these circumstances, we do not feel we should be justified in affiliating these aphorisms to Pañchaśikha.

44. Paṇḍita Râja Râm has, we observe, arranged *his* aphorisms of Pañchaśikha in a particular order, and has explained them in a connected form. This may mislead the unwary in thinking that this collection of aphorisms is a complete treatise composed by Pañchaśikha which, however, it is not, and can, by no means, pretend to be. To avoid any such misconception, we have, with the single exception of the first one,—and this, for obvious reasons—presented the aphorisms just in the order of their quotation by Vyâsa ; for there is no more reason known to us for placing them in one particular order than in any other.

45 It may also be just mentioned here that some other views, not aphorisms or sayings, of Pañchaśikha have been referred to in the Sâṃkhya-Pavrachana-Sûtram also. See *Ibidem* V. 32 and VI. 68; and Vijñâna Bikṣu's Commentary on I. 127.